You

Are A

GENIUS

*It's Not Where You Are,
It's the State You're In*

by

Dan Wedin

ISBN: 978-1-7349830-1-2

You Are A GENIUS

It's not where you are, it's the state you're in.

Table of Contents

You Are A GENIUS

It's not where you are, it's the state you're in.

Preface

Before diving into the Foreword and exploring the power of your thoughts, your habitual behavior and the fascinating science of the myelination of neural pathways, I'd like to express something of great importance about the way you read this book. Or any book you pick up from which to extract actionable intelligence.

In our digital age it's been noted that we tend to read differently when the words are displayed on a digital screen as opposed to the printed page. There's an apparent tendency to skim this digital copy rather than reading it comprehensively. I know this is true of myself and after reading about this a bit, online, I did in fact note that I was "skimming" the article. Caught me.

So I applied some additional focus and re-read the piece. Then read it to myself out loud. Intriguing, as suddenly the depth of the meaning conveyed was magnified. Definitely an area an avid reader such as myself wants improvement in. We'll be touching on "Deep Practice" in the course of this book, and I suggest you consider as you delve into it beginning to improve your "Deep Reading" techniques. It's a skill that will serve you well in the future and perhaps give you a competitive advantage in your field of endeavor.

Way back in those wild seventies, nineteen-seventy-five to be exact, a Hungarian-American psychologist named Mihaly Csikszentmihalyi observed a mental phenomenon he termed "flow". We've all been there, haven't we? We're so deeply entranced with something that the world falls away and we're singularly absorbed in whatever it might be at that deeply focused moment.

I contend that it is in these moments that the work we describe as "genius" can occur. This is the state in which we can advance our skill, widen our knowledge, gain profound understanding and make great progress. And perhaps reach great conclusions. And the best thing about this flow state is it's not like the mundanity of work, that dull drudgery we all dread. It's a higher plane, a more exciting existence, and a zone into which we want to return again and again.

And I gently suggest that you approach this deeply focused reading of this book with great and joyous curiosity. In these pages are perhaps doors leading to greater understanding of how your mind works, and how you can make your mind work for you to your great benefit. Don't just skim, dive deeply into the concepts and where you find mental movement, dive a little deeper. Don't be averse to rereading portions that "speak to you" and ignite a reaction in your brain.

Often the first brush with an intriguing thought is like the sprouting of a seed. Don't inhibit that force of nature, use it to your great benefit by nurturing its growth. As the sprout spreads its branches and leaves and its trunk thickens and roots deepen it will flourish in the vast expanses of your neural pathways. New knowledge! This will spark an electrical and chemical event in your conscious brain which will soon be implanted into the gardens of your subconscious. And it is here from which the fruits of your newly gained knowledge will ultimately come to life. Vivid, colorful life.

You're going to be thinking anyway, so why not grant yourself an upgrade to first class thought and study? This will inevitably lead you to first class action and accomplishment. Why not? You deserve it and always have.

Mindfulness is a popular pursuit in our age as it answers a need. Let's face it, our mental forces are too often scattered, aren't they? When our amygdala and hypothalamus (in a very complex reaction) are feeding us cortisol our brains are not engaged in much more than deciding whether to fight or flee. Let's see if we can avoid that stress-causing chemical reaction save for those most necessary moments.

Make focus sessions a priority, and include one whenever you're reading this book. Shut down your world temporarily and just concentrate on one thing. Do that one thing well, and then move on. It's a habit you shall not regret and it will quantify the advances you make mentally in all that you do. Whatever you're doing, be there for it, and be there with all of the focus and intensity at your disposal at that moment.

Time is limited, we all have an understanding of that as in our organized society we're surrounded with clocks, digital readouts, calendars and reminders that time marches inexorably on. In the interest of making the most of that most precious commodity, consider "Deep Reading"; something requiring no additional time, just more focus and single-mindedness on the matters at hand. Whatever and wherever they may be. It's a habit you shan't regret adding to your repertoire.

And remember, *it's not where you are, it's the state you're in*. Let's just see if we can't improve upon that state and if you follow through with intensity, imagination and focus, perhaps improvements beyond your wildest dreams are possible. Give it your best effort! After all, Why Not?

You Are A GENIUS

It's not where you are, it's the state you're in.

Foreword

You are the sum of your thoughts. All that you are, all that you become, is the direct result of what you have thought. These are thoughts you may or may not have chosen. And most likely not chosen, at least not the vast majority of them. Though there are exceptions, mighty ones, among us.

Thoughts fly through our consciousness, seemingly unbidden, driven by the left side of the brain. And for some, the term "driven" describes a journey bordering on the insane. And at times all the way over the line. Think *"panic attack"*, a couplet seen with increasing frequency, and we can all relate. These can escalate to extreme dimensions, taking control of one's consciousness. Think *"road rage"*. Think any *"rage"*.

In her marvelous New York Times bestseller, *"My Stroke of Insight"*, author Jill Bolte Taylor details her personal saga of having a stroke and documenting each and every phase in clear scientific terms. Bolte Taylor, a neuroscientist, serendipitously becomes the ideal spokesperson for the journey she takes us on, all the while describing how the brain can be severely damaged and return to full vitality through the power of neuroplasticity. And emerge with more wisdom concerning the thoughts one chooses to entertain.

I highly recommend this book which I've read twice and will read again most certainly. Very illuminating and I'm thankful it was recommended to me by a relative. It simply fit into my research beautifully. A beautiful instance of *bonne chance*. So what's the goal of controlling or managing that stream of consciousness that is part of our makeup?

The calm, composed choosing of empowering thoughts produces what? Order, purpose, and an upwelling of good feelings. Who doesn't want that? An existence of purpose, of focus, of accomplishment; these are the hallmarks of a rich life, are they not?

Then why don't we all live like this? Are we too old by the time we realize the power of our own thoughts to change behavior with roots in infancy? Perhaps in the womb of the woman who bore us? Possibly, but let's remember that change is the only constant. And while there are consistencies to our thought patterns over time we age, grow, gain enlightenment, grow happier, grow less happy, face depression and a wide range of other feelings.

And if one believes as I do that *"the will to do comes from the knowledge that we can do"*? Why not exercise a wholesome control over our thoughts? If we can establish neural pathways of belief in ourselves beyond our often limited view of who we really are, then in concert with our will our potential exponentially increases. In fact, it can lead to a fuller flowering of one's human powers. And the world is a better place when more and more of us allow this amazing potential to reach full and vivid bloom.

One could make the case that in this era it's more important than ever that as many of us as possible are operating at as high a level as we can. The challenges are daunting, our forces are divided, so it falls upon those of us who clearly see the need for action to make up for those who choose to remain static. And we know from our history that at times it's one person who can shift the course for the better. May our fellow humans continue to step up in our moment of need.

And *"You Are A Genius"* is hardly the only means to this end of self-improvement. There's a library of books written on the topic and recorded thoughts that stretch back into ages long past. We get one shot at this life and to let time slip through our grasp without advancing our individual causes and thus the cause of mankind in general is unfortunate. But it doesn't have to be a source of regret for you, does it? I encourage you to reach for the sky, look life in the eye and be all that you can be until the day you die. It can add a great deal of excitement to your life, and is an internal journey rich with discovery and satisfaction.

The noted writer and speaker, the late Philip Laut, wrote once that *"bliss"* is our natural state. I don't know about that, it's never been mine, though I've certainly enjoyed my share of blissful moments and periods. But I liked his postulation and since the choice is ours? Why not?

Why not accept that changes are happening all around you and within you and intelligently direct that process of change to your benefit? I think it's a most worthwhile goal and has allowed me to exert a certain empowering and wholesome control over the tempest-tossed turbulence of my own thought patterns. Exercising this influence mentally is an interesting experience, and honestly, only you can embark on this journey, and no one can coerce you to do it. Simply a matter of choice. But that's not as simple as it sounds, is it?

Life belongs to the living, and he who lives must be prepared for changes.

Johann Wolfgang von Goethe, 1749-1832

I read a random response to something online once, and it struck me. And it rang such notes that I selected a pleasant font, enlarged it and printed it out. It hangs out of sight in our home but in a spot where we can see it frequently. To wit:

Joie de Vivre

"This is a beautiful way of thinking. As an existentialist, it is sometimes hard to see the meaning of life. The meaning I have found is hidden in the phrase "La Joie de Vivre". The meaning of life is to be happy and enjoy one's life. The only things that are worthwhile are those actions that will contribute positively to the world; to one's own or someone else's happiness. This communal selfishness will improve the world and one's personal life."

Who wrote this? I haven't a clue. It was posted on a website called "webot.org" in an online discussion of "La Joie de Vivre" in 2010 and it was anonymously left. I simply chanced upon it. I'd like to thank the author and would be more than happy to credit them. I really like it and it's an intriguing summation of how to find happiness. So if you can solve this myster-e, by all means contact me.

Yet we all have different needs and goals. But I would suggest you consider, amidst the sheer bedlam of life, that you dedicate part of your time to your happiness. We are calmer, more creative and more productive when we are happy. I invite you to follow a technique I'll share with you that possibly could launch a personal voyage of discovery to more happiness in your own life. Just follow the thoughts, go with the flow, and feel the wonder of one simple fact: Every thought you think changes you. For better or for worse. I trust you'll choose better.

And as your thoughts change, your actions will follow. Oh don't worry, you'll still be you. You won't be "brainwashed", unless eliminating or tamping down the senseless worries, aimless guilt patterns and the serial useless thinking we're prone to occasionally is your definition of the state.

When you're thinking an empowering thought another effect manifests itself. As your brain responds to these stimuli, and you'll have endless freedom in how you use it, it changes. Chemicals will be released that will make you feel good, bad, or indifferent. But in my experience the chemicals released by practicing the techniques in this book have been good. Sometimes really good, though by nature these are rather short bursts in most cases. And it takes some consistent effort, I'm not going to downplay that, yet what begins with purpose soon blossoms into a valuable habit. And dopamine, the great motivator, can spur us on to further discovery and enlightenment the more we delve into it.

And as we exert the effort to focus on one thought, one line at a time? A rather curious yet familiar force comes into play: Automaticity. Automaticity is the transformation of a behavior from a single event to one that requires no thought, and no discipline. It becomes like the breath we breathe, an almost involuntary response to being conscious. And perhaps even as we sleep.

Though I've found that when these thoughts course through my brain it does so with my tacit and conscious approval. Just as when a negative thoughts appears one can exercise editorial control and not just stop it, but counteract it with an equally powerful positive antidote. That's the genius in always choosing, and choosing wisely. It soon reaches a level of automaticity that makes it effortless to a degree.

The question for you to answer is how diligently will you apply yourself to these thoughts? Dedicate yourself to them and you'll soon find they become part of the vivid and varied patterns of your unique mentality. That makes it so much easier and at times very exciting. Changing for the better is key as change will occur whether you like it or not. To dedicate oneself to constant improvement is a very worthwhile course to pursue.

Will you now be a genius? Unless you're already working under that august title, no. But neither am I. Yet I've had a stroke of genius now and then and I'm betting so have you. What we're trying to do here is focus your thoughts and energies on changing the way you think. And once you've incorporated these simple habits into your daily life from morning to night, you'll find your mental attitude changes for the better. And invariably your sleep patterns and many other aspects of your life as well. And why not aspire to greater mental power and focus?

When you accept that your life's circumstances are a direct result of what you think, what you have thought, what you fear, what you're mentally attracted to or in the habit of focusing on, what happens? You're already a living example of the interconnected nature of thought and behavior. Thought and action. Thought and mood. Thought and accomplishment. And believe this: Changing the way you think for the better is one great accomplishment. Why? Because every single facet of your conscious life is directly connected to your thoughts. Think differently and you'll act differently and hence produce better results.

When you change your outlook on something it doesn't just effect a change for the moment. In fact, change what you think now will inevitably change what you think in the next minute, the next hour and profoundly affect what you think in the future. It's all part of the flow of your growth pattern. Imagine back to a time when you were faced with a daunting challenge of any kind. Were you to persevere in that effort and overcome the challenge, you could feel the change, couldn't you? More confidence, more inherent belief in your ability overcome anything; these instances affected all areas of your life as you grew.

Understand one thing: your thoughts are ultimately powerful in the quality of your existence. It's in the choosing of those thoughts that allows you to exercise that power. I've known this for many years, with modest results, having read the seminal *"As A Man Thinketh"* at seventeen. Over the ensuing years I read that brief, but profound work, dozens of times. And committed key quotes to memory.

"Act is the blossom of thought; joy and suffering are its fruits, thus a man harvests the sweet and bitter fruit of his own husbandry."

James Allen, (1884-1912) "As A Man Thinketh"

Though in today's enlightened age we would say "thus a person", or "thus a woman", wouldn't we? And though this concept makes eternal sense, the book stopped short of delivering a method that allowed one to control those thoughts. Still, we seem as humans, across the broad spectrum of our religions and philosophies, to have arrived at the conclusion that one should think good thoughts.

"The highest stage of our moral culture is when we learn to control our thoughts."

Charles Darwin (1809-1882)

"As a man thinketh, so is he."

Buddha (5th to 4th century, BCE)

"Finally, brethren, whatsoever things are true, whatsoever things are honest, whatsoever things are just, whatsoever things are pure, whatsoever things are lovely, whatsoever things are of good report; if there be any virtue, and if there be any praise, think on these things."

Philippians 4:8 King James Version (KJV)

"It is not the eyes that are blind, but the hearts."

Quran, 22:46

And because we seek to control our thoughts, to a degree, this can be a centralizing force for our imagination. Just as the magnifying glass takes sunlight and focuses it to a point where searing heat is generated, so can these techniques bring your disparate thoughts to a tightly focused point and perhaps spur you to action, or at least a different state of mind. It is not where you are, but the state you are in that makes life what it is beyond the ephemeral and transitory trappings of time and place.

Understand that I have no interest, generally speaking, in changing what you believe or what you hold dear. Those are sacred freedoms and that is not my goal at all. My goal is to simply provide a structure through affirmations, or "affs" I'm going to ask you to say to yourself whenever you want. Or skip it, it's your choice. But by saying these on rising and settling down for the night and at intervals during the day you'll heighten their impact.

You want to consider thinking about what you've read and stay curious, and continue to think the thoughts, mind still open to the possibilities. By the time you're a few days into this book and its suggestions, the ones I practice every day, you'll note changes. I find it brings me great happiness and peace, things which have not always been my strong suits in life. Yet amor fati. Love your fate. All of it.

And a beautiful thing about *"You Are A Genius"* is that once you have this elegant tool, you can make it your own. You can customize it. You can improve it. In fact, one of my great hopes is that some of my readers might take this and discover a new and better way, a yet more adroit model that improves and enhances the thoughts of your life. Because in the end, what you think and what you feel is your life at this moment. And this moment, when all is considered, is all we truly have.

I am forever a student plumbing the depths of my ignorance. And as any dedicated student with humility will attest, the further one gets in the search for knowledge the more humbling it inevitably becomes. So why not seek the wisest sources by studying the giants of thought in our collective past and those of a more recent vintage as well as many other topics. And everyone I meet seems to have something to share of value, even if it's a warning of dangers ahead. At one end of the spectrum we can set a wonderful example, at the other we can provide a horrible warning.

Finally, there's great potential between your ears. If you could but focus that incredible mind of yours you could do almost anything! I was a radio spot writer at one point in my writing journey. When challenged with a major account project I'd sit back and ask myself what the best spot, based on all I know, would be for this client. And then forget it. Radio spot writing was my version of getting paid for enjoying myself. One great idea can take on a life of its own.

So once the cue was given to my subconscious via an adroit question, I'd go off and do something else, follow some other trail. Once I was challenged by the marketing director of one of Ka'anapali's finest resorts during their tenth anniversary. She stood up and drummed her index finger on the desk, demanding I come up with something fabulous as there were many other execs from the chain in the LA area where the schedule would run. It was a pleading-command.

I felt the pressure but following my ritual I went back to my room, changed into trunks and headed for the pool. I lay in the sun, asked myself what I could write that would fill the property and turned to other things on my mind. And we always have plenty to think about, dream about, and plan, don't we?

I returned to my room after five, changed and retired to the sushi bar off the five-pool layout. I had a few laughs with a young Japanese couple whose five-year-old boy stared at me as if I'd escaped from the zoo. They were eager to find out why I added wasabi to my soy dipping plate, mixing it in. I asked if they didn't do that in Japan.

The husband told me no, as the sushi chef already had seasoned the nigiri with wasabi. I don't know whether that's true or not, I've not traveled to Japan, yet, but I looked at the pieces on my platter and shook my head as I could see no trace of wasabi. He instructed me to lift the strip of raw ahi from the rice and lo and behold there was a smear of the fiery root. So I tried the next piece with just a touch of plain soy sauce and it was beautiful. He smiled, she smiled, the little guy smiled. And I did, too.

I explained that we Americans often did things to excess with seasonings, meal portions, etc. And I told them I liked the fiery palate effect of the wasabi and that in large enough doses it triggered the release of endorphins in my brain which are an opiate-like chemical that gives one a euphoric feeling, aka the "runner's high". They looked shocked at first and then laughed and I laughed with them as that was about as close to the "runner's high" as this avid walker would get.

Then I headed down the beach and did a bit of people watching and stopped at a couple of other bars with which I was familiar finally hitting the hotel's "Beach Bar" whose bartender was a local who closed the bar each night and then went fishing in his small boat to return early AM and deliver his fish to a buyer. I found my room just after midnight and immediately retired for the night and was soon fast asleep.

At 3:10 AM I bolted up, noting the large red numerals on the alarm clock. Grabbing the stick pen and little pad on the nightstand I began to write. I was done in less than five minutes as a thirty-second spot is less than a hundred words. I neither thought this up, pondered it, or had any idea what I was about to write when I sat up and put my bare feet on the carpet.

And when I awoke the next morning it took me awhile lying there to recall I'd even woke during the night. When I looked at the handwritten script I actually had very little recollection of it. But it flowed, and it drove home the point beautifully. I later added the voice-over close, got client approval and produced it. Guess what?

Its run in LA was so successful for the property they scheduled additional stations and lengthened the run. The property's website and phone bank were busy, the resort filled up and my client was a hero. Sometimes the magic works. She moved on at a certain point to a more prestigious property on a different island and invited my wife and I to enjoy a visit on the house. It was lovely and brought the process full circle, reinforcing my belief in the power of a timely question posed to the subconscious.

So science, the media and our personal experiences have hopefully taught all of us that focusing our thoughts results in focused action and thus the desired result, right? Set your mind on something and your chances of attaining your goal vastly improve. And while a focused approach enhances your odds of success, we all know as well, that there is no guarantee of success in anything. But every attempt at anything worthwhile yields valuable knowledge. And over time focusing your thoughts in an organized method on your goals produces another result. You find the skill transfers. To everything. That's a good thing in the theater of life.

Once you begin to lead a focused life there is no knowledge or plausible goal out of your reach. When your goal is in focus with your thought patterns and you don't let it go, suddenly all of your attendant activity is intricately designed, subconsciously and consciously, to produce that most desired result. I've seen it happen, I've felt it happen, I've made it happen.

More from *Goethe*, the famous German writer and statesman; he put it this way:

Knowing is not enough; we must apply. Willing is not enough; we must do. Whatever you can do or dream you can, begin it. Boldness has genius, power, and magic in it. Few people have the imagination for reality.

And another sentient thought from *Goethe*:

Concerning all acts of initiative and creation there is one elementary truth — that the moment one definitely commits oneself then divine providence moves too.

Now let's see if this simple habit can work for you. But first I must warn you. There are a million techniques and paths designed by us humans just waiting to be tried. Look at college. You can send one person to college and they can learn, and learn to learn leading to a life of achievement and glory. Another student, immersed in the same institution can wash out, lose interest. While another can complete the courses, get a job and tread water for years. Life is highly individualized. And education is not a destination, it is a journey, a life-long journey for the more one learns the greater looms what one does not. What perhaps one will never know. *Ask the best questions you can along the way! Why not?*

And most dangerously a student can enter an institution of higher learning with its impressive architecture and gifted professors and complete all of the requirements for a degree, get the sheepskin in a ceremony with a definite air of finality and accomplishment to it, and stop. They're now "educated". The need for additional learning has been largely satisfied. Finally, they can read for enjoyment!

And yet the knowledge they've gained is a transient thing, and while those strict requirements have indeed been met, there was no dictate that one had to actually remember all of that massive knowledge load consumed under pressure in compressed fashion. And the learning grinds to a halt save those lessons needed to be learned to earn a living. After all, they're *"educated"*. Yet education is not some mental box we fill, it is a door we open and stride right through, observing, asking questions, taking mental notes, building on and sometimes questioning deeply what we "know".

But as the sage noted, knowledge without love is a dull, cold, lifeless thing. You downloaded a lot of data but did it land in a network capable of assembling it in an orderly fashion? Did you arrive at any life-changing conclusions? If you learned to ask questions, to be skeptical of just about everything until you own it, you're on your way to educating yourself. And importantly understanding the implications of said knowledge and seeking further depth to add to what was gained.

No schooling was allowed to interfere with my education.

Grant Allen, 1848-1899 (Also attributed to Mark Twain)

And if you're no longer a student in that effort you are perhaps missing the greatest adventure upon which one can embark and that is understanding. And if you understand it all, stop here and please, write a book as the world needs your advice. And that includes me for there is much I've yet to understand. I have many questions. Endless questions. One of my favorites is, *"How good can I make this day?"*

So as is true in so many of the myriad paths of life you'll traverse, you'll get out of this what you put into it. I can't change that. But have hope. I am one of the least organized, laziest people I know. At one point in my life I recognized my plight. I was a hedonist. And I used to joke that with my own style I was a "Wedinist".

But the reality is we're all alike in so many ways. We'd rather be online shopping, reading about our favorite team. Following the political drama of the day. Or deeply ensconced in Game of Thrones or an enthralling novel, or a thrilling, all-consuming online game.

The real joy of "You Are a Genius" is that once you begin, unless you pull out early and abandon any thought of pursuing this path, you will find benefit. The words will become ingrained in your mind until you find lines just springing up as you begin walking. Or as you stretch, or practice yoga.

This is exactly why I wrote this book. I know of so many incredibly talented people that lead lives of great merit. Yet the focus required to do something really special is not there. Perhaps this tool can elevate their game. It did mine. This world, as in just about every age of humanity, needs saving. Needs improving. Needs elevation to a higher purpose.

And whether we are aware of it or like it or not, our brains will continue to pour forth a stream of consciousness that can be the most confoundingly disparate set of thoughts one can imagine. *"You Are A Genius"* can take some of that ongoing cacophony and silence it a bit, (or as my Father used to admonish my brothers and sisters and I, "Keep it down to a dull roar") replacing it with empowering thoughts directed at making you happier, healthier, wealthier, more confident, less stressed and stronger.

And a funny thing happens when you take this journey. Those dominating thoughts wither when displaced. That's a very welcome respite and a profoundly productive result. Conscious thinking of the good will help you supplant the bad.

Come with me. All I ask for is a bit of your precious time. Grant me that and let's see if by standing on the shoulders of the Thought Giants that have come before we can do one simple thing: *Every day in every way get better and better.*

I believe in you. Partly because I know the vast majority of you are smarter, more industrious and more ambitious than I. And we're off! Especially me, but I'm getting better. And I expect you to, as well.

To close this introduction, I'll warn you. The human brain resists change. The "rut" we often hear referred to is actually a set of neural pathways and once established they're immensely easy to return to. We just think that way, it's what sets us apart. It's the joy and sometimes the sorrow of our existence. But those can be changed as you'll soon discover through using the power of repetition and expectation.

But we'd be mistaken to discount the staying power of established thoughts and feelings. But we definitely can change and we do change, anyway, whether we intend to or not. We're just trying to direct that process of inevitable change and it doesn't take that much effort, actually. Nonetheless, it might be wise to convert that obstacle to a conveyance with this aff. I'm inserting my name here but suggest you consider while reading this through the insertion of yours:

I am a genius applying my wisdom so that every day in every way I embrace change.

Dan, you are a genius applying your wisdom so that every day in every way you embrace change.

Dan Wedin is a genius applying his wisdom so that every day in every way he embraces change.

These lines are a variation on a theme established by Emil Coue, a French apothecary and psychologist who discovered the medicines he delivered to his customers seemed more effective when he raised the expectations of their effectiveness. His work on this theory helped further understanding of the *"placebo effect"* which is the result of belief in a prescription of any kind. Often a sugar pill can be as or more effective than a medicine being tested. Once approved, the reputation of that medicine, the branding, advertising and labeling all play into its relative efficacy via the placebo effect.

By law, the FDA cannot approve a medicine unless it's been shown to be more effective than a placebo. Thanks, Senator Estes Kefauver! Turns out, due to the immense power of expectation in the human mind, that this is very difficult to accomplish with certain conditions. And while it's a hindrance to getting medicines approved which protects us all, for our purposes it is a force we want to employ to advance human thinking and achievement.

You're going to start out, save a few wunderkinds out there, slow. The untrodden path in the deep forest of your mind can produce excuses, procrastination and delay. You might even feel stupid saying this to yourself but you'd be ignoring centuries of thinking and observing to not forge ahead. As the first few steps in the morning can often be a bit unsteady, soon we're gliding through the day with ease, thinking great thoughts to meet each moment with vigor and enthusiasm.

So it is with the launch of this personal self-improvement project. But you only have to begin it once and with that behind you there's a certain effortlessness to it, as there is to an athletic skill you've repeated over and over until *"muscle memory"* takes over, which is, in reality, a well-myelinated neural pathway and not muscle memory at all. It's just memory. Think of this as just skill and once these simple lines are etched into the myriad paths of your subconscious you'll hardly need to think to entertain these powerful lines which you'll find quite profoundly valuable to you.

I was lucky. I suffered a bout of congestive heart failure that resulted in cardiac arrest. I was felled by a racing heart that stopped. It had to be restarted. And was so undependable, by my cardiologists' assessment, that it could not be left to its own devices. So they installed a defibrillator and a pacemaker in my chest above my heart. On the short drive home after a week in the hospital the morphine drip wore off. I was fatigued, I was listless, I was in severe pain, I had little ambition beyond sustenance and little zest for that. When I thought of my dreams I would see them in resignation as they sailed away without me in my mind's eye.

I was looking at a shortened life of questionable quality. And yet my brain kept repeating, often involuntarily:

Every day in every way I am getteing better and better.

Every day in every way, Dan, you are getting better and better.

Every day in every way Dan Wedin is getting better and better.

And I did. I found myself doing things involuntarily that were good for me in addition to following my doctor's medicinal instructions. Eating a heart-enhancing diet. Taking supplements well known as heart-helpful. Never quitting, Refusing to settle for a twirling descent to an inevitable bottom.

And something else happened worth sharing. When I'd struggle, and it seemed a constant companion, occasionally I'd just want to lay down and not fight it. And somewhere far deep inside I'd hear myself firmly telling me to get up, to move on, to go forward. When my thoughts turned defeatist I would hear *"Stop that!"* and it would shake me out of the fog and back into motivating thinking. And I imagine that kind of reaction was propelled by my personality but also by the endless drumbeat in my brain that there were better, more energetic days ahead. The wonder that is expectation.

Every day in every way, almost, I got better and better. Stronger, more energetic, more confident and more optimistic. When I visited the cardiologist next I was doing better and each subsequent visit charted an improving patient. "Keep doing what you're doing!" I was told more than once. I owe them the credit, but they couldn't have done it without me. And to the cardiologist that gave me five years to live? Thank you. I now try not to look too much further beyond five years down the road. That date in the future was seared into my neural pathways forever.

Yet I marveled at how those two years had affected my habits. Avoidance of exercise had become a ritual, a game at which I would always win. That had to go and saying Coue's line proved it inevitable. And the gratifying feature of the process is that the neural pathway one is faithful to grows stronger and stronger.

This led me to walk more and more, run in place, lift some weights, park away from entrances and just break free from the ennui deep fatigue burns into one's brain. It was soon in my wake but not before I acknowledged that it was evident that I could succumb to the lure of that rut and never emerge.

Your will to do something often springs from the knowledge that you can do it. I'm telling you right here, right now that you can do this. And as you change just a small portion of your daily thought patterns you will feel different and better, and your actions will inevitably reflect that new reality.

Today I feel better than I did ten years ago. And I'm not done...because every day in every way I have every intention of getting better and better. At least for the next sixty months! And once I returned to full health the thoughts continued to flow. Now *"getting better"* would occasionally mean my physical being, but it also transformed into just getting better at everything I was doing and all that I sought to accomplish.

If you're in the throes of a physical liability, I encourage you to augment your current regimen with what I'm going to lay out before you. And if you're already healthy, you have a head start on a voyage of good feelings, internal peace, and motivated actions toward whatever you desire. Establish the habits and unlike many self-help books in my wake, these empowering thoughts will stay with you long after this book's gathering dust on a shelf somewhere. *Give it your best thought.*

For as you forge ahead you will be blazing new neural pathways as the electrical connections are made and magic myelin wraps the thought path with feeling and emotion that makes returning to that thought familiar and stronger. As each chosen wrapping of the myelin around those nerve fibers establishes its power, and given focus and discipline in one's thinking, it wraps ever more layers, making that channel one where the thoughts and feelings associated with it grow ever more vital and voila! Effortless. Nearly.

You'll still have to consciously return to the empowering thought but with each myelin wrap it will grow stronger and the thought will come easier. Soon the thought loops associated with this chosen thinking will return to your consciousness again and again, begging you to follow that path, think that thought, and build the connections that amount to the skills you'll need to succeed on your chosen path.

Myelin's the magic, but you are the magician. Think the thoughts, focus on your goals and as you reach each one you'll make the realization of your particular individual dream closer and more fulfilled. For every thought you think changes you, a theme you'll experience again and again. Choose wisely and your wisdom will be rewarded. You can do this as any clear-thinking person can. Yes, you can do this and don't hesitate to profess that, to believe that, and to practice the life-changing thinking that will elevate you to the existence you desire. So onward and upward we go.

"I know what I have given you. I do not know what you have received."

Antonio Porchia, Poet (1886-1968)

Let's find out what you've received, and by the time you're done with this book you'll know. Simply provide the focus and intensity and let *"You Are A Genius"* provide the thoughts that will enter your conscious brain and by the time you're done the process of their entry into your subconscious will have begun. You will own these thoughts. The more intensity and focus you deliver the more progress you will have made. I have high hopes for you. High hopes.

Your mind and the thoughts you think are yours and yours alone. They are your personal kingdom. ***Rule it.***

You Are A GENIUS

It's not where you are, it's the state you're in.

Chapter One
Welcome to One Man's Happy Death

I pulled into the parking lot at Mike's Drive-In in Sellwood, Oregon for lunch on Veteran's Day, 2016. Mike's was closing soon and a couple of friends and I planned to bid it a tasty farewell by having their legendary "Mike's Special", a super-deluxe combination of grilled sesame seed bun, fresh quarter-pound beef patty fried crisp, Tillamook Cheddar Cheese, peppered bacon, fried egg, lettuce, tomato, onion, pickle, with house-made Thousand Island Dressing. It fit the *"Greater than the Sum of its Parts"* criterion I'd employed for years when it came to a good hamburger.

We greeted each other, placed our orders and caught up on the many lines that intersected in our lives. We were all in high anticipation of the last of the "Mike's Specials" at that location we'd be enjoying that overcast autumn day. I took my first bite, and stopped breathing. Completely.

No, the hamburger didn't kill me, as some have suggested, though it was one killer burger. That's old science, a myth from the past. And I didn't see it coming, though I'd been diagnosed with "Congestive Heart Failure" some time before, and was on medication to treat it. Yet I had no issues with arterial plaque accumulation as later tests would prove.

The two guys at my table thought I was joking at first, but soon realized that I was in the middle of a medical crisis as my face turned blue. They moved my leaned over and inert form to the floor and instantly two women in the restaurant recognized my plight and sprang into action. One began performing CPR but not as vigorously as the other thought was necessary to revive me so she pushed her aside, reportedly saying, "No, harder!"

She proceeded to jam at my chest, severely damaging my sternum and cracking a few ribs. My face had turned darker blue and the emergency medical technicians who'd responded to the 9-1-1 call estimated I'd been "dead" for six minutes based on the time of the call and their arrival. It's estimated that after five minutes your brain starts to lose its oxygen supply which can spell the finish.

They ripped open my shirt (which I've had repaired and still wear occasionally; ironically, it's appropriately solid black silk, my "Death Shirt") and shocked my heart with the electrical voltage (200-1000 volts) of a mobile defibrillator. According to a witness my body jumped violently in response to the high voltage. It worked, my still heart re-started.

My face, by all reports, was returning to normal coloration and I was breathing. Later I'd recall a vague memory of being across the room viewing the frantic scene playing out on the floor at Mike's. I wondered if someone was having a heart attack. Recounting this later my wife and daughter looked at each other and said, *"Out of body!"* Perhaps, the memory came from somewhere and maybe it's a good thing the incident happened in a place that smelled so good. My spirit was possibly lingering just a bit before exiting the premises. But I digress.

I recall the overcast light coming into the back of the ambulance as we raced to the hospital. The road seemed unusually rough but it was all overshadowed by the EMT in my ear, shouting, *"Stay with me, Dan! Stay with me, Dan!"* I remember mumbling something about not going anywhere.

We arrived at Providence Hospital and much of those first few hours is an indistinct series of images. My wife's face, filled with concern, was one thing I recall. I couldn't, but wanted to tell her not to worry. My credibility was on its back and nearly unconscious at that point, though. Might have been the morphine, the shock; I really don't know.

In the ensuing hours I slowly returned to as full a consciousness as one can enjoy on a morphine drip. And in retrospect I've nothing but good things to say about the dosage level. I had no sense of being in pain until it was cut off when I left the hospital. Then, yes, the damage to my ribs and sternum was an ever-present reminder that my body had gone over the edge and been yanked back, violently.

On the second or third day of my week in the hospital, a cardiologist appeared at my bedside. It seemed like two or three times an hour some member of the staff appeared and they were wonderful, every one. The hospital stay was remarkably enjoyable. I had a lot of laughs and the food? Hospital food has come a long way and their cuisine was comfort-food-delicious. Especially the Zenner's Chicken Breakfast Sausage with Granny Smith Green Apples. Just a little shout-out there for a Portland shop that's been around since 1927.

Anyway, the cardiologist smiled and said, *"So you're the miracle baby"*, while looking at a chart.

I confessed to confusion, understandable under the circumstances. I was neither a baby nor could I link any miracle to my condition. He proceeded to tell me that ninety-plus percent of Cardiac Arrest victims die on the spot. And that the majority of those who survive, less than ten percent of all victims, mind you, experience brain damage.

He then explained that I'd passed all of the cognitive tests and exhibited no damage. Such a relief yet it was odd, I hadn't even worried about that. My wife has expressed her concern since that day that modern science cannot yet determine brain damage in cases like mine. Funny, Honey. And an unfortunate sign that my sick sense of humor's permeated her sweet and kind demeanor. Such a shame. Yet I digress again.

I had a history of strong belief in the power of thought, triggered initially by reading *"As A Man Thinketh"*, by James Allen at age seventeen as I've noted. And I'd read it repeatedly over the years to the point that I often quoted lines that struck me as important. The little tome never changed, but with each reading I could sense that I had. A phenomenon I've experienced with many books since.

And I'd continued reading other books on the topic, all of which spoke to me, he who needed self-improvement. And once you read a book that you can feel changing your thinking somewhat for the better, that ignites a burst of positive brain chemistry and lights up a neural pathway, you're on an endless treasure hunt. It delivers the impression that perhaps there is that one exhilarating line, that one philosophy, that will produce peace of mind and the focusing of one's personal forces.

So I had a love for elevating thoughts, those that had much more quality than my usual mammalian-heritage-survival-mating-matrix with all of its resultant actions and feelings. I yearned for control, I sensed a higher plane out there somewhere, and I was, in all honesty, quite jaded on religion. That so many faiths proclaimed theirs as the "one" struck me as proof that all were worthy of suspicion. As if magically one's birthplace put them in line for their "true" beliefs. And a few of the proponents seem highly suspicious as well, especially those who make a career out of passing the televised collection plate.

Yet I decry most of them not, and have known and know many to whom faith is a critical touchstone and belief in their lives. To each his own and this book was never intended as nor is it an indictment of any faith anyone chooses for their own. It can simply be an adjunct and perhaps a force for deepening said faith, whatever form it may take. And there is a smorgasbord from which to choose, isn't there?

And with the book which follows this personal account of an incident that serendipitously inspired it, I have no desire to change who you are. That is a sacred decision, in my mind. But if it can serve to help a few people elevate their thinking, focus their overall thought patterns and deliver an existence richer with satisfaction and happiness? Well, there it is, I ask for no more.

I am not a scientist. I don't have glittery educational credentials. But I am a curious person and an enthusiastic autodidactic, and have written all of my life whether it's in making a living or just for the pure joy of the thing. Yet, as writers are often wont to do, I rely on the science as described by those dedicated to any number of disciplines. And I admire them, as one with an aversion to just about anything requiring discipline. Yes, I'm your lazy brother-in-law, the one more likely to be composing a song or poem on a cocktail napkin than sending you a nice Christmas card.

My Father was a newspaper editor and publisher who studied journalism at the University of Washington. He owned a newspaper, "The Fishermen's News" dedicated to coverage of and advocation for the west coast commercial fishing fleet from San Diego to Dutch Harbor. At one point he was a UN Law of the Sea delegate. In 1966 he went to work as a professional staff member on the Senate Commerce Committee for Sen. Warren Magnuson (D-WA), who was chairman, with his lifelong goal to establish a two-hundred mile limit which would regulate any and all foreign fishing fleets in our waters. He succeeded with the "Magnuson Fisheries Conservation & Management Act of 1976", aka the "Fish 'n Chips Law". I'm sure he enjoyed a huge rush of positive brain chemistry when the president signed that into law.

He charted his progress along the way, step by step with a wall calendar behind his desk to which he'd affix shiny gold stars to certain dates. Hearings completed, important support gained, etc. Later, much later, I'd discover the value in the celebration of achieving goals on the way to accomplishing a dream. But that's for another portion of this book.

He often told me to *"Get it right"*. I took it as gospel in a way I took little else and the older I grow the more difficult I realize it is to make those three words ring true consistently. We live in an ambiguous world of knowledge that grows and changes endlessly with the line between opinion and fact blurred disconcertingly. Those three little words echo in my brain frequently and I feel my Father's presence. Repetition has such great power for good and at times, evil. But we're going to use it for good, aren't we? Yes, we are.

So back to my Cardiac Arrest vignette. I had arrived home, the morphine had worn off, and the glow of what I thought was gratitude for surviving faded away. Though once I got ahead of the searing pain box that was my chest, I occasionally admitted I had been lucky. Very lucky, not just to have lived through it, but to have survived with my faculties intact. I told people I had *"...died and returned to heaven."* And I wasn't kidding. I had much to be thankful for on my worst day, and a Life and Family to celebrate on my best.

I'd been diagnosed a couple of years earlier with Congestive Heart Failure and was still trying to understand the implications beyond its life-threatening nature. And the research continues in the wake of this dramatic event.

I felt the pain during this period, screaming out occasionally when making certain movements, even through the pain-killing effects of my Vicodin prescription. A morphine drip it was not, but I resisted the temptation to go beyond the advised dose though there was a time or two when I took one an hour early. Had to, and I had the feeling that just trying to get through a day without it would be painful enough to cause me to pass out.

Who knows, but perception is reality and I felt that sense of being broken and fragile and wanted to get past it as soon as I could. And one night at the table I coughed, painfully, and did pass out for a few seconds. When I awoke my wife had her phone in hand dialing 9-1-1. Shaky start to a recovery but I was determined.

Throughout this saga, from day two in the hospital, morphine-addled as I was, I had a recurring thought, born out of the teachings of the aforementioned Emil Coué (1857-1926), the French psychologist and pharmacist who had developed a psychotherapeutic self-improvement technique based on optimistic auto-suggestion.

Every day in every way, I'm getting better and better.

Every day in every way, Dan, you are getting better and better.

Every day in every way, Dan Wedin is getting better and better.

Say that to yourself right now for the first time, out loud if circumstances allow it, inserting your name for mine. Hopefully this will be the first of many times those lines course down a developing well-myelinated neural pathway in your brain. Myelin is the result of thoughts and experiences that ignite neural fibers in our brain and this myelin in turn coats the fibers, which adds up to "skill", as I've noted. More on this later but feel free to do your own research. This is game-changing, life-changing science. But the important thing to remember is that it must ignite, there must be an element of urgency, of inspiration, of focus.

I had begun thinking this triplet a number of years before and found it gave me a good feeling, think positive brain chemistry, and it seemed to inform my choices favorably. But now that I'd been felled by a foe it leapt to the fore as if my subconscious was telling me, *this is the path back to where you were.*

And I set out on that path and have not wavered for one day since. Oh, certainly some days I say it with more intensity, some days I see more results, but in *"deep practice"* that's to be expected. And I must note, they are all "good" days. That's just a product of cultivating gratitude and we'll get into that more deeply down the line as well.

And to clear something up, it's not like I didn't know the congestive heart failure was affecting me. I felt different and not better with it. I was fatigued and battled that mentally and with perhaps a bit too much coffee. I also had requested a cardiologist appointment sooner than the early December date they'd scheduled. I was told they were all busy.

In frustration one day I asked what I was supposed to do if my heart gave out. Go to emergency, they said. It seemed dangerous and indeed it was. But I'm not here to indict the system, just to make the point that each one of us has to take responsibility for their own condition. Go with your gut instincts, your subconscious speaks in feelings sometimes, not words, so trust that deep feeling. It might save your life.

On a previous visit to a cardiologist she'd dismissed my questions about getting my heart back to normal. I found this disturbing. I asked her then, if I couldn't cure congestive heart failure, how long did I have? Five years is the average, she said, unemotionally while looking down.

I left that appointment feeling a kind of tired defiance. I shuffled down the hall, swollen edema-stricken legs and all in a pair of Birkenstocks whose soles were not seeing the light of day and whose belt-like closures were on the last available hole. And I could only wear my Birks and really stretchy socks as my triple-E's were alarmingly oversized.

I dragged myself across the parking lot feeling I was an exception to the rule. Looking back it seems slightly humorous as I was definitely not looking the part. I looked like I belonged in a hospital. It wasn't the first time I'd had doubts about my medical care. Once I had a kidney infection and had been put on a series of antibiotics for nine months when I was with a different health system. First three, then when it reappeared, six months more.

I didn't realize it at the time but I'd completely destroyed my microbiome, something few were talking of in those days. When I developed an irritating and distracting skin rash on my legs, feet and arms I asked for help. They gave me a prescription for hydrocortisone. I researched that and discovered it wasn't recommended for longer than two weeks. I'd already been on it a month and didn't really want to encourage the side effects that apparently were well known.

So I seized matters into my own hands. I took action beyond my insurance health network and sought out a naturopath which I paid for as my coverage would not. In my first and only session with her she asked me dozens of questions. After about half an hour and a quick exam she told me I had a yeast infection. I said what? That's a woman thing, isn't it?

No, she told me we were all subject to them and they were more common than most believed. She recommended I cut down on the bread and beer and take yogurt daily as well as a probiotic. I followed her instructions and within days began to see improvement. It took some time, years actually, but I had begun the process of rebuilding my microbiome and have now almost completely eliminated the condition. In a true sign of progress this naturopathic doctor is now part of the system that treated my cardiac arrest's "Integrative Health Clinic". Good. We're learning, aren't we?

I've explained this to a medical professional or two and they've been skeptical. But I've since read that research is pointing to a weak microbiome as a novel cause of cardiovascular disease, not to mention skin conditions. Your microbiome is home to seventy-plus percent of your immune system, after all, so it's a factor that affects you head to toe.

I've taken that to heart, as it were, and pay strict attention to this important aggregation of bacteria. The brain is equipped with up to one hundred billion neurons; some days I take in twice as much of that in good, microbiome-restoring bacteria of various strains. After all, the microbiome is home to trillions of good and bad bacteria, and in a healthy state all play a role. And research has revealed the "gut-brain connection" via the Vagus Nerve, indicating the health of your microbiome has a profound influence on your mood and cognition.

So I consult, but I remain skeptical, do my own research, and chart the results. But in this case it was more serious and so I followed instructions to the letter. When it seemed like I was just in a holding pattern I sought more help. I researched and read, dug into databases, followed the discourse from alternative medicine figures, often ones at odds with the medical and pharmaceutical establishment, and asked a lot of questions. And for some of them there were no answers.

Then, as part of my continuing research I read a book called *"Anticancer"* by Dr. David Servan-Schreiber, and *"Stroke of Insight"* by Dr. Jill Boldt Taylor (as previously noted) and many others, including the one from Dr. Coué. And some ideas began to take hold.

This is the story of where those ideas took me and how one thing and one thought led to another and another and on and on. Today my heart numbers according to my last two visits with my cardiologist are "normal". I feel better than I have in years. But this is not a health book, per se, as you'll soon see. Though the potential impact on one's health is undeniable, though everyone's results will vary based on a myriad of factors.

Let me share with you what I've learned, and continue to research. The brain is one frontier we're exploring the world over and the results hold great hope for our future progress as a species. And frankly? We and the rest of the beings on the planet are counting on us to do better. It's my great hope that this book and the thoughts contained herein will continue to help me do better, and you as well.

In the second chapter we're going to launch into the thought pattern that elevated my mental attitude toward recovery in a most exhilarating way.

To finding the Genius that lies within *You*.

Dan Wedin

Chapter Two
Some Thoughts on Thought

What Do You Think?

We all think, don't we? Sometimes we focus and sometimes we just ride the wave of never-ending memories, impressions, fears, longings, music and brain chemistry-triggered sensations provided by the greatest computer on earth, the one nestled snugly between our ears.

Yet we must not rest on our laurels, work is underway to create artificial intelligence that will surpass our cranial capacity. It will happen, and that makes the individual maximization of our mental capacities all the more urgent. And we live in a world of wonder, yes, but one also facing a Covid-19 Crisis, a Climate Crisis, environmental degradation, inequality, war, hunger, hate, pestilence, cancers and other diseases and on and on.

Yet we do have the mental capacity and wherewithal to solve all of man's ills, don't we? If we but focus and work together. It starts with better, more powerful thinking and human wisdom. So what's happening in our brains?

Is there more going on there than just attending to the matters at hand, planning for the future and remembering the past? Of course, there's dreaming of what might have been, fantasizing about what still might be possible. And that reaching beyond the possible to what seems impossible yet is still highly pleasurable to think about.

Hopefully this book will help you create a mindset that shifts many things that you now view as "impossible" into the "possible" column and eventually into the *"I Can Do This"* seats. And right on through to the *"I Did It!"* section reserved only for Winners, who stand before us with brains bathed in the occasional exhilaration of our innate brain chemistry. Momentarily, though, before wanting "more". That's just part of who we are physiologically and psychologically.

Now back to your thinking processes. Sometimes there's just wallowing in self-pity, sorrow, anger, regret and other Byzantine plots whose source is shrouded at times in mystery and surrounded with riddles, isn't there? Okay, I hear you, let's throw a conundrum or two in there as well. And the occasional "quandrum", a recent addition to our malleable and growing language. It's an organic entity, after all, with each word a portal into history, cultural idiosyncrasies and human progression.

So what's my point? My point is that I ask you to consider the possibility that you could focus that thought-stream and direct it so that you would sometimes, at first, find yourself in the right place at the right time engaged in the right activity. And then do it with greater consistency. And that which you were doing could work out more beautifully than you ever imagined on a more frequent basis. And enjoy a deep, compelling sense that you were on course, moving confidently ahead while achieving your goals and realizing your dreams.

Sound impossible? Then read on, and if you're unable to see the possibilities for you at this point in your life, it might be more challenging than it has to be. After all, tell me you can do something plausible and I'll give you my full support. Tell me you can't do something and well, I'll tend to agree unless I have some self-interest in changing your mind. Check your mindset and if it's pessimistic, hopefully the next chapters will help you see that it's just a mindset, not a permanent condition. And optimism is the springboard for moving ahead, lifting yourself up and believing you can do things that pessimism currently prevents.

It's been estimated we think in the neighborhood of seventy-thousand thoughts per day, and up to forty-thousand of those can be more or less negative in nature. In a world that can veer into negative, stressful and threatening territory at times who needs a whirlwind of negative thought plaguing us from within? Especially if we have the means to supplant those thoughts with much better ones chosen specifically to strengthen us, to enlighten us, and to enable us to lead happier, more peaceful and richly satisfying lives.

So, of course, I encourage you to consider giving it a try. An honest-to-goodness, best-you-can-do try. You've already bought the book, after all, and I can tell you from my personal experience the potential for you is perhaps even greater than the profound effects I've experienced. We don't get unlimited time on the planet and if, as the "Stoics" recommend, you should base your thoughts and actions on the thought that this day may be your last, it makes urgent sense. For if every day in every way you're getting better and better? So is your life! And your contribution to the lives of those you love the most.

All my life I've been fascinated by self-improvement books. And few needed improvement more than me. I owe my Mother some credit here. She bought me that beautiful Hallmark edition of *"As a Man Thinketh"* by James Allen when I was seventeen. We weren't on the best of terms at the time, I wasn't even living at home, but on my first reading I was thankful as I noted in the foreword. It's a succinctly written work just teeming with good thoughts, deep truths and inspiration. And I know my dozens of readings helped steer me in the right direction and provided solace in trying times. It became a kind of bible to me and many of the phrases stuck. For good.

And then a few short years later a friend gave me *"How To Be Your Own Best Friend"* by Bernard Berkowitz and Mildred Newman, a gifted pair of married-to-each-other psychoanalysts. That was also welcome, helpful and a candidate for re-reading at certain times. And once you do become your own best friend life is just a lot better and you discover you're never alone. I would point to that book as perhaps the one that illustrated how unhappy I was at the time, though unable to truly admit it and come to grips with it. Yet it gave me a push toward new thinking and thus new and better feelings. And spurred me to both recognize and come to grips with my haunting sense of impending doom.

I used to travel a lot for a media firm, logging hundreds of thousands of miles and HTBYOBF and its tenets made that ever more enjoyable. I was no "lonely traveler", but one engaged in a constant conversation with myself fed by new places and endless curiosity about the locales I visited and the people I met. And the foods! Oh, the wonderful array of fabulous foods.

"Nothing, to my way of thinking, is a better proof of a well-ordered mind than a man's ability to stop just where he is and pass some time in his own company."

Seneca Died, 65 A.D.

Next, my Sister, Deborah Ann, sent me a copy of *"Money Is My Friend"*, by the late Phillip Laut. Now that's a fun book and it's about a lot more than money. I was marketing director at the time for a radio network and it just made me so much better at helping people with what we were promoting. Mr. Laut teaches you that when someone says "No," what they're really saying is, to paraphrase, I love you, I respect you, I honor you, and I look forward to doing business with you in the future.

That line made me laugh out loud when I first read it, and I'm smiling now. Powerful way to disarm rejection completely. A powerful and potentially dangerous mindset, as one can imagine. But worth exploring just to push rejections aside. And it's a thought we'll revisit later in this book.

I also read *"Pyscho-Cybernetics"* by Dr. Maxwell Schmaltz. Another valuable work. A line stuck in my head: *"I will fight with all my might to make my greatest life goal battling for self-respect."* I'm certain a re-reading at this point in my life would prove valuable so it's on the "Re-reading List".

In high school a late friend's father handed me an old copy of *"How to Win Friends and Influence People"*, by Dale Carnegie. I was a new kid in a coastal town having moved from the big city. I found it fascinating and its tenets rang true. I saw a lot of my Dad's personality and style in that book, especially the statement that the sweetest sound in the language was each individual's name. In his paper he always printed the names in bold type, each and every one. I could see the affirmed value in that.

They're all good, frankly, and all have great value for those trying to improve their mind, their life and increase mental focus and elevate one's attitude. What works for one may not for another. We are a highly varied species when it comes to our minds due to a richly textured set of well-oiled (think "myelinated") neural pathways. Yet all seem to provide great value if taken seriously and studied carefully to extract the actionable intelligence.

But none of these books really produced the change in me that I sought. I wanted transformation, I wanted something that day by day would produce measurable change that I could feel. I like to tell people that we don't have to remake our world today, but if we can make incremental advances day by day it spawns hope and optimism and bursts of dopamine in our brains, fueling future efforts. The law of compound interest works with sums of money and it works yet more profoundly in building mental wealth and power as well. It's the wisdom behind the Japanese practice of "kaizen", where seemingly small yet strategic changes made as problems come to light add up to *"getting better every day in every way"*.

So when I discovered the late Emil Coué's *"Every day in every way I get better and better"* it gave me hope. It made me feel good. I could see that, in fact, I was doing some things differently, better, and I liked that.

The Epiphany

But it wasn't until I allied it with *"I am a genius, applying my wisdom so that every day in every way I'm getting better and better,"* the results were more dramatic. The practice of that one line in the I-You-He format literally exhilarated me. It elevated my mood and focused my energy. I could feel the brain chemistry rush it inspired the first few times I went through the "I, You, She/He" series and a splash of dopamine upstairs is again, a great motivator to continue that behavior.

37

It's all part of our primal urge to survive, without which some other species would be ruling Planet Earth. Though some might say "ruining" Planet Earth and I wouldn't fight them on that in this era. One of my great hopes is that this book may inspire some involved in battling the Climate Crisis to find new inspiration and focus.

The encouraging effects of *"I am a genius applying my wisdom every day in every way to getting better and better"* seemed to become part of the very fabric of my thoughts, displacing those that did little more than occupy my time. Or worse, lessen or even doom my bliss. I didn't know it at the time but I was simply experiencing the myelination of a neural pathway carrying this thought with ever-increasing urgency and skill.

Coué's book, *"Self Mastery Through Conscious Auto-Suggestion"*, is available in all of the usual forms, including audiobook. The Amazon listing for the title provides the following encapsulation:

"The Coué method centered on a routine repetition of this particular expression according to a specified ritual—preferably as much as twenty times a day, and especially at the beginning and at the end of each day. When asked whether or not he thought of himself as a healer, Coué often stated that "I have never cured anyone in my life. All I do is show people how they can cure themselves." Unlike a commonly held belief that a strong conscious will constitutes the best path to success, Coué maintained that curing some of our troubles requires a change in our unconscious thought, which can be achieved only by using our imagination. Although stressing that he was not primarily a healer but one who taught others to heal themselves, Coué claimed to have effected organic changes through auto-suggestion."

His short work is rife with examples of cases of disease and physical disablement that were alleviated through the power of thought. The pen is mightier than the sword and perhaps at times, via auto-suggestion, the thought is mightier than the medicine. But I am not, under any circumstances, suggesting anyone use auto-suggestion in lieu of needed medical care. I'm a firm believer in regularly scheduled visits with one's primary care physician. I discuss everything with my doctor, and have kept him informed of progress on this book, in fact.

Yet if following these thought rituals empowers, strengthens and energizes one's attitude, it follows that crafted strategically they can also enable this self-healing process within. It's certainly seemed to improve my health, day by day, week by week, and year by year. I look back and am astounded at times how low I'd sunk and how much I've elevated since then. And the process continues.

So the more time we decide to spend thinking empowering and uplifting thoughts the less time we waste and the more and better results we'll produce. When you grow as a human being it's often a stop-start, two steps forward, one step back process, but over all it's progressive. With the *"I am a genius…"* preface? I felt excited.

So with the desire, a bit of deep practice and the automaticity it inspires, we find that within our brain grows glittering neural pathways lit up with electric thoughts and myelinated for endless repetition. Desire + Practice + Automaticity = Results. I was never a math whiz but that adds up to me as the process is deeply embedded in my mind. But I can do better and I will as the automatic nature means the mechanism is with me at all times and judging by how many times I wake up thinking an empowering thought, this includes my hours of sweet slumber.

And when it comes to auto-suggestion, the unconscious brain processes up to eleven million pieces of information per second as opposed to one's conscious mind which can process forty. So implanting these affs into one's subconscious delivers the automaticity that makes the practice so intensely more powerful than just consciously thinking the thought. This is a path, this is a way to focus the immense power of one's brain and its ever-evolving myelinated neural pathways so that suddenly you're underway on this exciting journey. And the automaticity in one sense amounts to momentum, which you can add to with the addition of consciously selected and strategically timed thoughts.

The question inevitably comes up, do I think of myself as a genius? Absolutely not. Do I aspire to strokes of genius, to moments of genius-like inspiration? Most certainly. It's all aspirational, isn't it, this desire for improvement, for expanding and enhancing one's talents? Does anyone ever actually reach their full potential? I'm not sure it's possible but it's a moot point, isn't it? The actual point is setting a course for getting better and better, every day in every way:

We win by becoming a better person than we were yesterday.

And the more I study history and biographies the more I have come to realize that those we characterize as "geniuses" largely don't see themselves in that light. Pasteur attributed it to "tenacity", Michaelangelo, on being called a genius noted that if only they knew the years of arduous work that led him to create the "Pieta"!

So the story of human genius appeared to me to be less the brilliant brain, though those do come along, and more just focused and consistent determination. A goal was set, a dream was envisioned and then the individual worked every day in every way to bring that worthy and lofty achievement to reality. And they did it with the intense focus of a laser guided beam helping ignite those synaptic reactions over and over. With essentially the same brain you possess right now. Though theirs were arguably populated with more myelin. Yours can be, too, as you'll see.

Within each one of us lies the seeds of greatness. I've seen this in action and it's particularly evident in the "brainstorming" sessions of which I've taken part. Genius ideas in a group are often difficult to source, but it's not uncommon for someone considered a lesser member of the group to make stunning contributions. Which promotes the concept of respecting everyone. *Everyone.*

It is a basic human need to grow, isn't it? As a child we yearn to "get bigger", as we want to reach our full physical potential. As we mature we continue this process by "getting educated" and learning of the world around us, especially those things which attract us, those things we sense we can master. With the dedicated and strategic use of the power of thought, we can position ourselves to grow in a myriad of ways. We can become a vessel for knowledge and then set our course equipped to launch great journeys and great efforts.

"You'll deserve the fortune that it will bring if forever reaching for your brass ring."

This is a line on a slip of paper I attached to a two-inch solid brass ring I found at an old-school plumbing supply store. I'd polish it up with "Bartender's Friend" with the slip attached and give it to friends and family. I personally carried mine in my pocket to remind myself to always be reaching beyond my present circumstance, to always be seeking a better way, a higher level of consciousness, and greater understanding of who I was and how I could serve humanity. And my self-interest, and that of my immediate tribe, of course.

Finally, all of the information and knowledge, all of the affs (affirmations) seemed to plug in behind this "I am a genius..." opener and come alive with new power. It was the loom I sought to take these disparate elements and craft a philosophy, and a way of living.

Millay's prose, written about humanity at large, also holds great wisdom for us as individuals:

Upon this gifted age, in its dark hour,

Rains from the sky a meteoric shower

Of facts . . . they lie unquestioned, uncombined.

Wisdom enough to leech us of our ill

Is daily spun; but there exists no loom

To weave it into fabric.

Edna St. Vincent Millay, 1892-1950

And this sense of our ultimate potential, once it takes hold mentally, impacts every waking hour and no doubt one's sleep as well. I cook better, I write better, I'm a better person. Oh, and I'm also more humble. Wink! But I do seem to love life with a more consistent intensity and it allows me to see a weakness and address it immediately. And at least for me the results can indeed be immediate. As an impatient American who wants instant gratification? It was the ideal.

But it takes consistent effort to achieve what's called "automaticity", where the empowering thoughts simply appear unbidden as you rise and navigate each day. They are your supporters, your reminders to focus, and your unerring companions serving as counterpoints to the flotsam and jetsam of one's daily thought patterns.

"Let me tell you the secret that has led me to my goal. My strength lies solely in my tenacity."

Louis Pasteur, chemist and bacteriologist (27 Dec 1822-1895)

And what Pasteur is passing on to us here is that he sees himself not as a genius as we do, but rather as one with an elevated sense of consistent purpose. And if the detritus of daily thought has you mired in neural pathways not moving you inexorably toward the achievement of your goals, the waypoints to achieving your dream or dreams, this lesson is key. Stick with it. Stay on task. Focus your energies and focus your thoughts.

What will happen is not the elimination of the paths littered with useless "weed seeds" acquired over the years, but the supplanting of those neural pathways with ones lighting up with synaptic firings which will, through consistent effort, be the ones where you will mentally live today and in the future. The choice is simple, and simply yours and yours alone to make.

I'm completely cognizant of the potential for some to use these techniques with discipline and suddenly feel different, more powerful, perhaps slightly all-powerful. This is good, but if they contribute to feelings of arrogance, stay mindful of that potential side road on this journey. It is a dead end.

So it may occasionally be of great value to say, "I am a genius, applying my wisdom to my humility", and so on. And I'm not only aware that this will be refined, improved and perhaps revolutionized, I humbly welcome it. For the use of these affs has not turned me into some super being, not at all. I'm just another person stumbling along in the human race. I still do stupid stuff, I still laugh at myself because I, like you, am not a finished product. And never will be. Yet I continue to aspire higher. Why not?

And it's of great value to view the events in your life through the prism of responsibility. When bad things happen to good people they find themselves dealing with their previously established neural pathways. They can feel like a victim, "It always happens to me!" or they can remain neutral and not fall prey to those debilitating thoughts and feelings.

Though it's very important to look at what happened for often the seeds of a negative event were planted by ourselves, and this is important knowledge in determining whether it's just an outside, uncontrollable event or one we actually can prevent in the future by avoiding planting those seeds of self-destruction. Taking responsibility for your life is healthy, but blaming oneself for an unfortunate occurrence outside of our control is not.

Things happen. People are going to do what they're going to do. It's just important to view them in the right light. It's not where we are, it's the state we're in, right? Make your state one that's healthy, strong, and self-supporting.

For it is in the journey, isn't it? And having good thoughts to accompany one through the topsy-turvy ride that is life is like having best friends along for the trip. You know them, but they always seem to be revealing a new side, and inspiring new thoughts. You will grow to love them, ideally, and you'll love what they'll do for your goals, your dreams and your overall mental health.

We face enormous challenges as a species threatening our own planet and our physical well-being. We need as many people on earth as possible thinking, working and acting at the peak of their abilities. Or at least at a higher level. Knowledge is power and improving our intelligence allows us to add to that knowledge dramatically. We don't just view new information, we process it, weigh it, incorporate those things of value and grow. And growth is exactly what I seek to inspire and enable in myself and others.

I believe this simple system can help produce that dynamic. And if it helps one brilliant person organize and focus their thoughts and produce stellar research that saves the life of one beloved child? I'll be happy.

It's not what happens to you or has happened to you that matters so much as how you react to it, of course. You lose your job for whatever reason. You can sink into despair, take it personally and view it as a career setback. Or you can accept it, dedicate yourself to conscious improvement, and begin instantly to explore an even better opportunity. So weigh your reaction, consider the opposite, explore alternatives. You know this, right? It's on the lips of the wisest with whom you cohabitate the planet. Take responsibility. All of it. And charge forward. "I am a genius…"

There will be times when you go through the affs and guess what? You won't believe it. Just keep saying it, focus on it, and deliver the words out loud with your greatest sincerity and emotion. This is you talking to you, after all. And it will pass. It can be like climbing a hill that's not a linear trail up, but rather one with dips and twists and turns and rocky, washed-out stretches. Keep climbing, keep persisting, encourage the "Tenacious You" inside and soon you'll look over your shoulder and down the mountain to where you began. And celebrate your progress!

Keep climbing, keep moving, keep thinking thoughts that inspire you and help you grow all the days of your life. It's not how fast you progress, it's that you persist in consistent progression. Just keep thinking empowering thoughts and soon they will simply be part of the fabric of your conscioius as well as your subconscious brain. This dynamic inevitably builds upon itself, opening new vistas of understanding and empathy and yes, even compassion for oneself for we've all suffered greatly in phases of our lives. But let's suffer once and not ad nauseam. We've better things to do, better things to focus on, don't we?

And when you hit that sweet crest and your senses are full and you're totally focused you can look back on that feeling and thank yourself for ignoring the voices that said, *"Give up, this isn't working, this is stupid."* It's not. It's part of the reasoning countless individuals have known and taught for thousands of years. It's your turn to leverage this wisdom of the ages for your own benefit. You will not regret it as it will help inform and activate all of the other wisdom you've gained in your life.

But here's something to keep in mind as you read this book. Where you find inspiration in the words, revel in it. Always seek and be fully open to inspiration in all of your waking moments. From the most disparate sources, our lives provide opportunities to discover the kind of inspiration that can deliver jolts of powerful and pleasurable brain chemistry that will vault you forward, and make the journey ever more exciting. After all, why not?

The more you do this the more you will strengthen (and "myelinate") those neural pathways and we'll discuss further the actual mechanics as we go along. They're an important new frontier in the exploration of human nature and how our minds actually work and how a so-called "talent" is actually developed. This is key knowledge that will illuminate what's going on upstairs as you live your life.

You are here, in the right place at the right time, and whatever challenges you face, they belong to you. You have the right to a happy life, to fulfill whatever dreams populate your conscious mind like hovering angels. Give those angels life and breath, they are the guides to your unique ideal life. And you deserve nothing less. If you don't feel that's true in your heart, repeat these affs until you love the thought, until you embrace the thought and are feeling the thought with your entire human being.

I am a genius applying my wisdom to the dreams I hold so dear.

Dan, you are a genius applying your wisdom to the dreams you hold so dear.

Dan Wedin is a genius applying his wisdom to the dreams he holds so dear.

Your brain operates on expectation and while some refer to dopamine as the "pleasure chemical" this is only part of the picture. Dopamine's triggered by the unexpected reward. You drop off a shirt at the cleaners and notice there's something in the pocket, a love note you'd intended to keep and cherish. Instant spray of dopamine with a chaser of oxytocin. And then it passes as it's reabsorbed. You're going to find that some of these affs will unexpectedly trigger that spray of dopamine which is, remember, the great motivator.

Yet over time the same aff will lose that impact which is okay. Just as revisiting that love note too often will blunt its impact. We're not doing this solely for the pleasurable rushes, nice as they are. But this lack of chemical response is natural and no reason for dismay. Once an effect is taken for granted that mechanism is not triggered and in some ways that's a good sign. You've incorporated the thought into your subconscious so it's time to move on to the next aff, one in this book or one of your own creation.

Seek and ye shall find the affs that answer the questions and defuse the weaknesses lingering in your conscious and subconscious. For at times they can be explosive thwarters of your progress. But you can return to that original basic "I am a genius..." aff, and using your imagination, reignite those synapses and continue the process of myelination. This is the path to automaticity that is so valuable and heartening to the spirit. Just do it with feeling, that's what it takes to light up and ignite that neural pathway.

It's all about incremental progress here and do not lose sight of the fact that as these habits form and inform your subconscious you'll be growing. And after forty-five days or more of this practice this will really become evident to you. But you'll see results much, much sooner. Persist, vary, imagine, explore; seek the chemistry that leaves you relaxed and calm and in inspired control. We're on a journey, you and I, equipped with a name we didn't choose in a place we had no say about.

We're literally "Shanghai'd" into this life in many ways, but once we're given this gift it's incumbent upon us to determine how responsible we are for how it plays out. And while fate takes a hand at times, as it were, we are largely the creators of our own existence. Make yours good, make yours all about the love, all about not fighting that dopamine-fueled desire for "more", to ensure our survival, but about seeking what you truly want in your heart of hearts. You deserve it. You always have.

Thoughts you think frequently, feelings you have frequently, reactions you just can't seem to avoid, all come barreling down neural pathways of often unknown origin. And once they become active some tend to stay that way forever. The chemistry inspires the neurons to make electrical connections and the paths become myelinated which makes your thinking that thought not just easy, but inevitable. In fact once the neural pathway's well myelinated that thought, that skill, will flow up to a hundred times faster. An incredible achievement so keep encouraging the consistent daily persistence to make this happen with the thoughts you wisely choose.

So by exercising a modicum of wholesome control over our thoughts in an organized fashion a castle of beneficial thought begins to take shape. Or should I say, neural pathways begin to take shape. These good thought pathways, built by habit, are part of being your own best friend. You are literally building a shining city of good thought pathways in your mind, one that will benefit you greatly in all that you do. And this shining city represents where you will live and flourish the rest of your days.

You are the monarch of this internal structure, this set of pathways, and while so much of what we think lies outside the walls of this wonder we seek to enhance on a daily basis, just having this haven to return to frequently is a comfort. I often wake and with my eyes closed find a thought coursing through my conscious brain, served up by my subconscious. Why? Because I found pleasure in it yesterday and want to return to that feeling again today. And it was so powerful it has become embedded into my subconscious. A very powerful thing indeed.

Many of us wake to a new day in a rather grumpy mood. We need our coffee, our juice, our tea, a glass of water, a shower, a shave, our makeup, a morning radio show; something that signals our brain to elevate beyond the lethargy that's so common in the morning. Particularly if one's in the habit of hitting the "snooze alarm". And I'm no exception.

For me it's coffee and morning radio and a shower. And an unfocused brain if I've made the mistake of waking and then returning to sleep. That shot of glucose our brain reserves for our own survival's been spent so consuming something to replenish the glucose, the brain's fuel, is not a bad idea. For me it's blueberries and yogurt but to each their own.

But I've found that just the act of thinking, "I am a genius applying my wisdom to getting better and better every day", has grown beyond just a desire to get better so I could live, it now informs how I think, how I feel and how I simply exist. And it allows me to strategically tap into the great thoughts of the sages that resonate in my brain, so I don't just appreciate their wisdom, I make a sincere attempt to live them.

So I, too, obviously, am subject to the same randomness of thought as the rest of us mammals and probably more scattered than most. These affs just allow me to approach each day with a little more focus, and a little more direction in the course of my activities. And we all know that whatever it is we're doing, if we're doing it a little better each day it's reason for optimism and that can provide all of the motivation one needs to persist in the effort.

Try this before turning in tonight and try it a few times between now and then:

I am a genius applying my wisdom to getting better and better every day.

Dan, you are a genius applying your wisdom to getting better and better every day.

Dan Wedin

Dan Wedin is a genius applying his wisdom to getting better and better every day.

Every time you think this thought it travels down the neural pathway you've established for this line of thinking with these affs. This thought, when you think with focus and feeling fires a set of neurons which causes your oligodendrocytes and astrocytes to produce myelin (a phospholipid) which will wrap the nerve fiber and thus produce a "skill". But you can't just do it once or it remains one with which you've only toyed. Why do we want to take it past that point?

We want this myelination process on this neural pathway to repeat that over and over. And as the layers grow the nerve fiber will begin to look forever like a string of old fashioned butcher sausages, all linked together. The myelin coating can reach fifty layers if not more and as it becomes more than just a passing fancy, it becomes a true skill. And one is not born with skills, they're learned. And the level of skill is the direct result of the intensity of this learning process.

"Deep practice" is a term employed by the brilliant author, Daniel Coyle, for this process. His book "The Talent Code", if you haven't read it, belongs on your bookshelf. And his "The Culture Code" is also of infinite value. Use your well-myelinated neural pathways for reading skills to avail yourself of the knowledge he imparts. It's priceless.

The world's greatest musicians, athletes, artists, scientists, writers and anyone doing anything at a high level have literally myelinated the neural pathways associated with that skill. Often from a tender age. You're utilizing a myelinated neural pathway right at this instant with your reading skills, as I've noted. And if you're an avid reader who's learned to truly focus and absorb whatever you're reading you have a very well developed and well myelinated reading neural pathway. This makes reading much easier than back in the day when you stumbled over words, slowly gaining an understanding and slowly coating those nerve fibers over and over.

And if you never really mastered reading, and we all perhaps know someone whose fate includes this tragedy, that pathway just never got built very well. So reading's hard which makes learning difficult and most likely produces a challenging life. One lived behind a veil of ignorance that makes the revealing of that humiliating and painful. It's not hard to see why parents and schools stress the importance of this most critical skill. That neural pathway, this skill for reading and comprehension illustrates why for some school and studying is "easy" and for others extremely difficult.

So all skill springs from myelinated neural pathways in your brain. It's important right now to incorporate the knowledge that your skill at anything is simply the cellular insulation your thoughts and actions have grown on your neural circuits. So the key is simply to think the thoughts I've laid out here and inspire the wrapping of these circuits repeatedly. This will make the practice of auto-suggestion easier and easier until you've built the skill and begin leveraging it to your vast benefit.

This is why repetition is your friend and ally in building the talent for powerful thinking. And once you've myelinated this circuit it becomes a kind of highway, smooth and well paved and at some point it's as if a coat of oil has been laid down making travel on it, i.e., thinking, just so much easier than it is at the beginning.

We're talking about nothing short of developing a neural pathway for self-improving thoughts that, once established, can allow you to apply this skill to any plausible goal you set before yourself. Want to be a better reader? A better student? A better parent? A better leader? A better person? It's within your grasp if you'll but employ this knowledge to gain the power of believing in yourself and thought by thought, day by day, it will happen. Every day in every way you will get better and better at it as it grows ever more easy. And I like easy. As in "it's just a habit I have" easy.

Launch the thoughts, begin myelinating those pathways, coating by coating and feel the power you gain as the skill develops. But a word of caution. Don't just say the thoughts out loud or to yourself in a monotone manner. Feel the thought, think the thought, stir the emotion, let your imagination run wild, and muster all of the focus you can until the only thing at that moment that matters is that thought. This kind of primal focus coupled with repetition is the key to making great strides. And this elevated focus will carry over into all that you do and help you lead a more mindful existence.

And as you cultivate this neural pathway and it gets easier and easier an entire world of thought possibilities will occur to you. I wake up and start my day with thoughts that come to me automatically. It gives rhyme and reason to my daily tasks, it elevates my outlook, improves my attitude and fills me with a sense of wonder that there's nothing plausible that I cannot do. Are you ready to embark, to loose the lines which tie you to the status quo?

But remember, the nerve that fires gets wired, or "coated". Myelin doesn't respond to wishful thinking or sloppy behavior. It responds to deep practice of the skill, focusing on each word and a growing sense of the meaning of the statement. Focus with intensity and you'll experience the ignition necessary to spur the myelination which will build the skill.

Allow yourself to concentrate, perhaps at a higher level than you're used to, and slip into this state of deep focus where the world around you slips away and you'll be able to return to that again and again in this process. That, too, is a neural pathway you seek to myelinate which over time will make the practice not just easy, but automatic. Think of it as your automatic thought transmission. You'll start with a manual, and soon upgrade to an automatic.

Focus on the chapters to come, think the thoughts laid out, say these affs with emotion and intensity and do it somewhat slowly at first. Finish the entire book and and let's just see where this course of action takes you. For remaining static as a human is really not a course that can be sustained for long. Change is inevitable and there's no law that dictates constant improvement. That's a choice. Besides, staying static is boring.

Dedicate yourself to growth, to being the best you can be today, to think with ever-growing intensity and as the myelin wraps the results will follow. You'll have a simple objective and that's to just be better than you were yesterday.

And understand this is nothing new to you in practice, actually. Your brain is gray matter and white matter. The white is myelin. You've got neural pathways associated with every single skill you employ each and every day. So since you're going to employ the existing set and build new ones for new skills, why not direct this major force by choosing to build a neural pathway that will enhance and strengthen every other skill you currently own? And perhaps launch new skills, only this time you'll be armed with the knowledge that by focusing deep practice on that endeavor you'll be ever more successful in building the skill, whatever it may be.

To igniting your brain's myelinated neural pathways! Every day in every way. And building one heavily myelinated neural superhighway devoted to nothing but empowering and enabling thoughts. Your future self will Thank You. And don't ever forget that we live in the future, as this moment's a thing of the past in the blink of an eye.

The future comes faster than we may currently realize. Embrace it, and revel in the knowledge that with each thought you're shaping that future as a world with the potential to be the one of your dreams. The days are long but the years quite short so seize this moment in time, this moment of your life. It's there, and it's just waiting for you to seize not just this day, but every day hence. Why not?

"The place to improve the world is first in one's own heart and head and hands, and then work outward from there."

Robert Pirsig, American Author, 1928-2017 (Zen and the Art of Motorcycle Maintenance)

You Are A GENIUS

It's not where you are, it's the state you're in.

Chapter Three
My Oh Myelin!

Myelination, that synapses-firing inspired wrapping of a fat-protein, phospholipid sheet over nerve fibers in your brain's neural pathways begins at birth and perhaps prior to and continues throughout our life. This white fat-protein coating in various places in your cranium represents your acquired skills and the thoughts of which you're most likely very familiar. They are "you", after all.

And these skills you've acquired are physically represented in your brain as that white matter wrapping neural circuits that you've built based on thoughts, actions and reactions. How you walk, talk, read, write, throw a ball, swing a club or a racquet and everything else. Everything. These just don't happen without that tiny electrical signal which spurs the production and the wrapping of that fiber with myelin.

And no two brains are the same though we share many similarities, we humans. And when we meet someone with similar thoughts and skills we feel "in tune" with that person, don't we? Our brains recognize a certain compatibility, and since we're comfortable with familiarity, and like people that are like us, bonds are easily formed. These "bonds" are actually similar neural pathways well-myelinated with the thoughts of and exposure to this pursuit, activity, sport, discipline, person, persons or group.

This process proceeds at a feverish pace early in our lives as we familiarize ourselves with the people and the world around us and gain skills. As we learn to crawl, cry, utter unintelligible grunts and monosyllabic tones and as we faithfully note the reaction each engenders. Imagine the blast of encouraging brain chemistry experienced by a child taking their first steps in full view of their parents and/or siblings! That can be very encouraging, so hey! We want to do THAT again! And so it goes.

But soon the reaction's gone, the neural pathway is somewhat myelinated so while we continue to build our walking skills and acquire further myelination we move on to other things we deem vital to our survival. Like running. One's more likely to ignite a synaptic electric connection created by the realization that a thing or activity is vital to our survival. And these things we instantly assess with amazing alacrity.

Such as getting to that fabled cookie jar Mom keeps on the counter! What youngster doesn't believe at a certain age that they could survive on cookies? I fervently believed it and spent as much time during the holidays sneaking red Santa and green Christmas Tree-shaped butter spritz my Mom baked and the variety of delights my Gram made for the holidays as I could. And no one at the dinner table would ever imagine I'd eaten a dozen or more cookies on the sly since lunch.

After all, our primary urges deep within our brain stem, our so-called "lizard brain", are for survival first and procreation second. Everything else, all of the trappings of culture and civilization, follow these two pillars of our existence, and drivers of our thoughts. We have well-myelinated pathways devoted to these two issues and the more one understands this the less mysterious our urges and actions seem. The processing assessments happen with such speed as to be nearly instantaneous.

It all springs from a simple, intuitive process of learning; and perhaps we've over-thought, regimentalized and defended the wrong system, the "conventional wisdom", for centuries. But not all of us. We have no doubt been overlooking the vastly superior methods employed by some of the greatest athletes, musicians, artists and other luminaries in history and down to the present, assuming it was just "talent", a "gift" the individual was born with.

Yet we now know it involves intense practice, the noticing of mistakes and their corrections, firing a chain of neurons that get coated repeatedly by myelin, the brain's white matter. This can make the movement or skill infinitely faster, more precise and well-timed. We call it "talent", sure, but in fact it's a learned skill, and the acquisition methodology is one that we can employ to our great benefit personally and revolutionize teaching just about anything as well.

Our *"Miracle Brain"*, as the best-selling author, Jean Carper, termed it, in her book of the same name, processes millions of bits of information per second. Without this blindingly fast survival skill one could easily postulate that we'd be long gone as a species as more powerful predators took the top spot on the food chain. Yet they didn't. Not due to our speed, strength, vision; those were inferior to species after species, but due to our cranial capacity and infinitely clever methods and devices ever-evolving to ensure the survival of the Homo Sapien populations around the world.

So we have this tool, this knowledge of myelin, and now what we want to do is build a vibrant and expanding neural pathway glittering with strategic and focused thought. Throughout this book, and of course in your personal auto-suggestion deep practice, insert your name for mine. And bring all the focus and concentration you can muster to bear here:

I am a genius applying my wisdom to getting better and better every day.

Dan, you are a genius applying your wisdom to getting better and better every day.

Dan Wedin is a genius applying his wisdom to getting better and better every day.

There. If you've really focused on just these three thoughts by saying them to yourself or out loud, you're launching a neural pathway, and begun the process of coating the neural fibers with myelin. Do it in all earnest, with all of that intense focus. If it's not much at first, don't despair. Just go with the flow and do it. With practice and time your concentration level will incrementally increase until you find you are at one with the thought, in an almost mesmerizing way. Mesmerizing. Now there's a word with a story behind it!

Franz Mesmer was a highly influential German doctor who lived between 1734 and 1815. I won't go into the entire story of his life but it's, ahem, mesmerizing, as it were. He preached a theory of magnetism that was more tied to his hypnotic presentations than science. He was the toast of Paris, a favorite of Marie Antoinette just prior to the French Revolution. And in an interesting historic intersection the most colorful of our Founding Fathers, Benjamin Franklin, weighed in on his social and professional fate as our fledgling nation's ambassador to the court of Louis the XVI. Mesmer was sent packing back eastward.

Today the term "mesmerizing" is most commonly associated with hypnosis (but can also mean fascinating), the often discredited but now very respected practice of deep concentration.

I owe finally quitting the nasty habit of smoking cigarettes, something I thought entirely impossible, to self-hypnosis. Quite startling to me at the time as I had no intention of actually quitting. But I did and it forever altered my view of the power of deep concentration. And now serves, for me, as a marvelous example of a well-myelinated neural pathway whose origin lay in watching my parents smoke as well as movie stars, television stars and sports heroes. And yet I succeeded in supplanting that habit with a new one: Breathing without a lit cigarette in my mouth or fingers.

The hypnosis practitioner, working with a crowd of seven hundred, didn't eliminate the neural pathway for smoking, he simply supplanted it with one featuring us as "non-smokers". And the use of that specific term was key as it was a positive as opposed to the dreaded "quitting smoking" and all of its attendant self-deprivation, anxiety and discomfort. No one wants to exist in that state for long thus smokers try again and again to rid themselves of the addictive practice.

Previous attempts at cessation hadn't produced a non-smoker, they'd simply produced a smoker who wasn't smoking. And who wasn't comfortable in the least with not satisfying that neural pathway so well myelinated with the ritual I'd often find myself putting out a cig I had no recollection of lighting. Think "road hypnosis", that familiar phenomenon where one finds themselves there with no recollection of the drive, especially acute when the destination's familiar.

I got so bad near the end that in the face of those who wanted smoking banned in the building where I worked I became known as a "militant smoker". And a proud one at that. One Monday I came to work and put my briefcase down and then stood, transfixed at what I saw. My cubicle contents were gone, replaced with someone else's desk, photos, and office supplies. My first thought was, "The jig is up!"

I retrieved my briefcase and headed to my boss's office. When I expressed my surprise she apologized and fibbed that she "forgot to tell me" that the San Francisco division had grown tired of the clouds of cigarette smoke drifting over their six-desk cubicle on its way to the cold air return to the north.

Okay, I said, thanks, mind racing, this was survival, after all, and headed to the two-desk cube and directly under that large cold air return was my desk with everything in place. Including the giant amber, six-notch ashtray that I kept at least half full of smelly butts. I look back with a bit of horror. And there were times during conferences over schedules with the scheduler that I'd smoke two cigarettes simultaneously, much to the disgust of this decent human being who'd headed up the anti-smoking coalition.

During the morning members of the San Francisco team would walk by, smirking, or making a snide comment about my new "view". They had "won" in this little intramural office game, I had to give them that. So when they all donned their running gear for a lunchtime run I decided to forego my lunch with office mates down at Molly McGuire's and instead dine in. My chosen lunch? My beloved "Kipper Snacks", a product by Beach Cliff Seafoods that were simply oblong tins of smoked herring fillets with a handy pull-ring top.

I opened two cans slightly and then took them over to the vacant San Francisco office and proceeded to drain the somewhat oily and definitely pungent liquid into all six trash cans under and next to the desks. Mission accomplished, I returned to my new space and enjoyed a lunch of herring fillets and soda crackers, smug in the knowledge the "Smokers" had struck back against the tyranny of the opposition. Definitely had a bit of Mad Magazine's "Spy vs Spy" flavor, or should I say scent, to it. This was smoked herring liquid, after all.

Soon they returned, all red-faced and panting as I sat next door working, having a cigarette, of course.

"What's that smell?"

"Where's it coming from?"

I chortled slightly and the SF area went quiet. I had shared my little gambit with a few of my fellow smokers who thought it was hilarious. And some soon dropped by the SF team with comments.

"Working on a fish catalogue over here?"

"Hey, you guys need to shower after your run!"

I loved it. But soon a delegation appeared and not a happy one. I explained that I liked my new cube, it had a window, and could see the wisdom of having a heavy smoker right under the cold air return, etc. But that I didn't appreciate having the move made behind my back and would've acquiesced agreeably given the choice. They seemed skeptical but I could see they, too, knew what they'd done had been surreptitiously. We settled it and remained friends.

But I knew that we didn't have the numbers to hold them off and when word that the president of the company favored the move, and he smoked, I knew it was just a matter of time. It was happening around the country and hey, I read the papers, as the information superhighway at one time was paved with pulp and ink.

If you're one of the thirty-four million Americans who smoke cigarettes acknowledge that there are sixteen million of your fellow citizens struggling with a smoking-related illness. And some are dying painful deaths even as you read this line. If you'd like to leave cigarettes in your wake, try this triplet:

I am a genius applying my wisdom to becoming a healthy non-smoker.

Dan, you are a genius applying your wisdom to becoming a healthy non-smoker.

Dan Wedin is a genius applying his wisdom to becoming a healthy non-smoker.

Will it move you to stop smoking immediately? Of course not, anymore than me saying I plan on spending more time in the gym in the new year will make me more fit. Yet if I follow through on my gym intentions and apply myself I most certainly will achieve a higher level of fitness. And actually that's not a bad idea, making a note here.

So no, it will not instantly cure you of your nicotine addiction. Yet I contend if you say this in deep earnestness every day ten times especially before retiring and on rising it will aid you in achieving that goal. And as the idea flourishes along a neural pathway it will become better and better myelinated and you will begin to find yourself doing what it takes to stop. So while yes, it's possible that for some it might spur a quick reaction for most it will be a route to the goal assisted by other thoughts and actions to that end.

Back to focus and concentration. Try these affs:

I am a genius applying my wisdom to my personal powers of intense focus and concentration.

Dan, you are a genius applying your wisdom to your personal powers of intense focus and concentration.

Dan Wedin is a genius applying his wisdom to his personal powers of intense focus and concentration.

When I was recovering from my cardiac arrest and saying my three lines throughout the day I found myself changing the nature of my rather hedonistic diet to one rife with vegetables, fruits, strategic supplements and increased green tea and water consumption. I didn't have to make a list of the changes to my intake I intended. I just found myself unerringly making the right choices and mysteriously avoiding those gluttonous episodes with three scoops of ice cream and lunches that while satisfying and pleasurable were not good for that person in my brain I pictured as "getting better".

The automaticity of this behavior I found effortless and encouraging. Act is indeed the blossom of thought and now I could see the direct correlation. Change the thinking and the behavior becomes inevitable. Just as anything one dwells on in fear soon seems to manifest itself in one's actions. The two elements, inevitably, become synchronized for better or worse. Note how we often unconsciously bring about that which we fear most.

Have you ever felt out of sorts? Just not feeling as good as you may have hoped? Sometimes we think this is time for a vacation, a change of pace, a divorce, a new job, a new place to live. Anything to escape this awareness that we're not feeling good about ourselves. So instead of some external change, let's leverage the internal workings of our brain by employing the power of auto-suggestion and build a sparkling neural pathway designed to do nothing less than make us feel better about ourselves:

I am a genius applying my wisdom to feeling better about myself.

Dan, you are a genius applying your wisdom to feeling better about yourself.

Dan Wedin is a genius applying his wisdom to feeling better about himself.

See how easy that is? Maintain a steady drumbeat of the original set of lines and then focus other lines on specific elements in your life where you want more. And again, keep in mind that wanting more is all part of our survival instinct. But do all of this thinking with intensity as your goal is to ignite that neural pathway, make those synapses fire and thus inspire the myelin to fly and coat, fly and coat. And the more layers of myelin you electrically inspire the easier this thought will flow and incorporate itself into your conscious life. And the results will follow.

But remember, and this is important. The wire (the neuron) that fires (releases on electrical impulse) gets coated (myelinated). So intensity, focus, emotion, imagination; bring all you can to bear on this thought process for optimal results.

Now it may sound like I'm suggesting you focus on these lines all...day...long. No, not at all. That would be impractical as we all have lives to lead, don't we? And if we didn't? Actually trying to do this for sixteen hours a day would drive one slightly crazy, I would imagine. And it's not necessary.

Just start your day with a strong set, and continue when it's convenient or when a thought sparkles into your consciousness and ignites the process. At times you may feel like your brain is bursting with it in excitement. This is myelination at it's best with the accompanying and encouraging brain chemistry. In my case I can hardly walk anywhere without these thoughts in various forms coming to mind. This springs from a period during recovery when I was walking daily to increase my wind and endurance. The words fall beautifully into the cadence of my stride. They lift my spirits, I feel the brain chemistry and a sense of excitement with the added bonus of the natural mood elevation walking can inspire.

Exercising, walking, running, biking; all are excellent times to let these thoughts flow. You may find it enhances your enjoyment of this fitness-improving practice. You're tied up anyway, right? And what are you thinking about? Why not double the benefit of your workout by exercising your body and your brain. Think of it as a total body exercise session. What a great habit to encourage and revel in!

So focus on the thoughts, ignite the process and let your myelin stores do their thing. Every day in every way you'll brighten and strengthen this neural pathway which you'll be returning to again and again. And soon? It will be an integrated part of your conscious life and you'll be on your way to increasing the myelin coatings where you want them, instead of where they've happened to form in the neural pathways of your past.

Think of it as your "Power Channel" as once you learn to choose your thoughts you'll enjoy a much greater control over your moods, your attitudes and ultimately? Your destiny.

"You have power over your mind — not outside events. Realize this, and you will find strength."

Marcus Aurelius, Meditations

You Are A GENIUS

It's not where you are, it's the state you're in.

Chapter Four
The Inspiring Nature of Habitual Behavior

One thing we know for sure is that we all think. Relentlessly. Our brains are busy from waking to sleeping every single day. And quite busy as we slumber away as well. So if you're thinking anyway, doesn't it make great sense to perform some quality control on those thoughts? To take command of as many of those thoughts as you can and direct them to the good? To the empowering? To the enriching? To your happiness?

Since you have to think anyway, and you will continue in that pattern without question, why not take a small portion of that time spent thinking and seed your thought process with grains of wisdom that will sprout and grow into trees, orchards, and veritable landscapes of powerful thinking? In James Allen's case, he likened the brain to a garden. Left untended it will soon be choked with useless weed seeds. But by careful choice it can flourish and bear fruit of great beauty and value.

It matters not which metaphor you ascribe to, does it? No. The voyage of the good ship *"You"*, a garden which you can shape and cultivate, a computer that needs a software update and the removal of some self-defeating malware; they all work, you simply want to select one that fits your personality and circumstance.

You're going to think anyway, so why not choose wisely? Selecting those thoughts that have powerful implications for your future. That lay the groundwork for living with an empowering base of habitual thought that you can use as a springboard for higher goals and a deeper understanding of your life, yourself and the world around you.

And let's be honest with each other here. Your bad mental habits are not just "you", they're just bad habits. And they come at a future cost in terms of outlook, health, your social satisfaction and the quality of your relationships. The most important relationship in your life, of course, is the one you enjoy with yourself. Though I've definitely had contact with individuals who do not enjoy that relationship with themselves, yet seem powerless to effect a change.

Yet it's there for them just as it is for you and me. The gardener is simply neglecting the garden. The ship's master is but asleep at the helm. The computer's plagued with malware and no one's undertaking the task of disabling the bad and installing the good. Where you are in the process is not nearly as important as where you aspire to be.

It Begins Again Each and Every Day

How do you feel each morning when you wake from your night of deep restful sleep? The latter's a bit of an assumption, isn't it, in this age where so many of us struggle with sleeping soundly? I have great empathy for those with sleep disorders having suffered through a period of "Sleep Apnea" when my heart was failing, it's a cruel affliction where drifting off to sleep has life-threatening implications.

Imagine having your breath stop when you slip beneath the waves of consciousness because you desperately, vainly, need to sleep! And to awaken in a full blown panic attack as if you'd just emerged from six feet underwater, desperately gasping for breath. To say it's frustrating is a gross understatement.

I was adamant about not succumbing to its effects, literally or figuratively and had a deep aversion to the CPAP routine, which I did try without success, though I recognize many rely on it completely in every sleep cycle. If you're suffering from any sleep-related malady, especially Sleep Apnea, seek help from your doctor who can refer you to a specialist if you have not already. This is key as sleep disorders such as this are dangerous afflictions.

So you wake up in the morning. That's a good start, after all, we only get so many of these opportunities to savor a day on earth with all of life's loves and wonders.

I suggest you consider launching a routine every morning with thoughts that will guide you to making each day your masterpiece of living. That is the goal, after all, and while initially you'll fall back into well-worn and familiar patterns, think heavily-myelinated neural pathways, you're changing bad thinking habits here one by one by supplanting them with better thinking. Do not underestimate the power of those well-worn neural pathways, though, just acknowledge that fact and set about the process of replacing them on your consciousness's main thoroughfare. To wit:

Every day in every way I get better and better at thinking good thoughts.

Dan, every day in every way you get better and better at thinking good thoughts.

Every day in every way Dan Wedin gets better and better at thinking good thoughts.

I am a genius, applying my wisdom to making every day work out more exquisitely than I plan it.

Dan, you are a genius applying your wisdom to making every day work out more exquisitely than you plan it.

Dan Wedin is a genius applying his wisdom to making every day work out more exquisitely than he plans it.

Or perhaps this will work better for you:

I am a genius applying my wisdom to making every day work out more exquisitely than I can imagine.

Dan, you are a genius applying your wisdom to making every day work out more exquisitely than you can imagine.

Dan Wedin is a genius applying his wisdom to making every day work out more exquisitely than he can imagine.

This is a good message to your subconscious that you're expecting a great day, and it sets a mental tone to help bring that about. Inevitably, learning to control your thoughts, to choosing your thoughts strategically and with all of your innate wisdom, heightens your expectations of a brighter future. And the "making everything work out" versions help eliminate the worries that come with planning anything as let's face it, many of us like to sweat the details. And since experience tells us that not everything works out as planned we can take a wider view of the entire experience and cast it as "good". Never, ever let perfect be the enemy of good in this ultimately imperfect experience of life.

If your perspective is always examining what's less-than-stellar you run the real risk of missing the stars around you. The people, the experiences, the sights and sounds and the unbelievable and scintillating serendipity that surrounds us if one is but open to the experience. So don't let a hyper-critical, judgmental and negative attitude rob you of the pure joy life is presenting to you each and every day. Just take it, love it and savor the good, the bad and the ugly. This is your life, after all.

And it's good to understand the amazing and powerful role expectations play in our existence. We go to bed expecting to wake up, don't we? Though some of us take it not for granted. Experiencing doubt about that which most assume is a given will enhance one's appreciation of that simple expectation.

So begin the process of reminding yourself daily that you expect your life and your thoughts along the voyage to get better and better. Why not? A static existence isn't really possible, given the rate of change in life, is it? So one either improves or slowly deteriorates. That's an easy choice to make when improving your life is a simple matter of establishing the habit of believing that every day in every way you're getting better and better.

Over time you'll find you're automatically programmed to make those subtle changes, those course corrections, almost like an auto-pilot on a boat, so that you're growing ever closer to your ideal destination each and every day. And you might laugh at how quickly these repeated thoughts become driven by automaticity which moves you ever closer to your dream state of being. So what is an ideal destination?

In "As a Man Thinketh" James Allen refers to it as *"the sunny shores of your ideal"*. So what is your ideal? Is it that dream job? A happy marriage? A prosperous business? Wonderful children? Finishing college? A flourishing love life? A vast and unending fortune? Travelling the world? Or how about just leading a happy, productive existence from which you derive great and endless pleasure?

The choice is yours and I imagine you already have the dream tucked away somewhere upstairs. Take it out, dust it off, and set your course for that port of call. You'll find yourself returning to that goal, adding more and more of the visualized pleasures you'll enjoy in that achievement as you think your way to your prized endpoint:

*I am a genius, applying my wisdom to living **my** dreams.*

*Dan, you are a genius applying your wisdom to living **your** dreams.*

*Dan Wedin is a genius applying his wisdom to living **his** dreams.*

It's really quite simple though if you had to discipline yourself to think this over and over, getting better and better at thinking it with emotion and sincerity, it would be quite difficult. But you don't have to and here's why.

In the beginning of the process it will take some conscious thought to get underway, to loosen those lines that have you tied to random thought and inaction and begin your voyage. But soon, you'll discover the immense power and irresistible momentum of this most valuable habit. Cultivating the habit of expecting yourself to think empowering thoughts helps you build momentum toward a higher level of thinking, acting and living.

And let's revisit Mr. James Allen for a moment. He writes that you must slay doubt and fear at every turn or they will thwart your progress at every step. So ponder any negativity arising from thinking these thoughts. You may not, deep down, think you deserve to reach this goal. This is bad code, bad thinking, a useless weed-seed that may have sprouted via some indiscernible cause, and it's holding you back.

The idea here is not to eliminate but supplant those less-than-worthy thoughts. And don't feel bad about the thoughts you think, we are all subject to the random and often negative thoughts our left brain has in store for us. Think of bad thoughts as a bad habit and learn to differentiate between thoughts you want to think and thoughts you do not under any circumstances want to entertain.

But as you continue to think consciously and repeat-repeat-repeat in many different settings and many different moods, you'll find it gets easier and easier. Those feelings and perhaps voices telling you it's not going to work, you don't deserve it, or this is not for you? As it represents that thing many fear to their core, "change"? Those forces begin to lose power. They get crowded out. So instead of these unproductive thoughts dominating you, you will dominate them with powerful, conscious thoughts and that's exactly what the power of good habitual thinking is all about.

You'll still have some of those bad thoughts in your mind, but you'll have taken over the main course of thought in your brain with empowering thinking that will inspire and delight you. An adventure such as this may, at first, be a series of defeats punctuated by small victories. Let the defeats go, celebrate mightily those small victories. You'll enjoy the rush of brain chemistry and it will spur you onward. The victories and their resulting mini-celebrations will soon crowd out the defeats as you build the habit of strong thinking and then those wins will come in waves.

Just stay on course and battle discouraging feelings as they are just doubt and fear which you *can* conquer. Give that incredible computer between your ears time and space and think good thoughts as prescribed and soon the mundane detail of having to remember to think right will fall away as you just simply think in this fashion every day in every way.

You can do it, simply have faith in yourself to change. Given time it will begin to happen almost effortlessly.

Your life has been all about change anyway, hasn't it? You grow up, you mature, you age; change is the relentless agent of your life. By controlling your thoughts you take this force which none of us are immune to and quite swiftly turn it to your advantage. Embrace change, it's your best friend, it's a source of hope and strength and growth. You can do it. Doubt it? What's in it for you? Try this:

I am a genius, applying my wisdom to directing the force of change for my benefit.

Dan, you are a genius applying your wisdom to directing the force of change for your benefit.

Dan Wedin is a genius applying his wisdom to directing the force of change for his benefit.

Feel slightly better? Imagine if you magnified that feeling until it was a raging storm inside you powering your every thought and action every day in every way. A brilliant writer scribed a thought once that ties into the now-realized fact that our brains come equipped with an internal storehouse of psychoactive pharmaceuticals, ready at our command if we but call on them. These are the chemicals that make you feel elated or sad, loving or mad, down and out or glad:

"Words are, of course, the most powerful drugs used by mankind."

Rudyard Kipling, 1865-1936

The journey of a thousand miles, as the saying goes, starts with a single step. Take that step, no matter how challenging it may seem to you at the moment. The second will be easier and soon you'll be confidently striding along, thinking good thoughts on the way to your ideal future, tapping into the best feelings your brain can conjure.

We're not seeking to remake your world in one fell swoop here, understand that. We're simply changing one little thing here and there, planting seeds, loosening the moorings of inaction. Whatever metaphor fits your mindset the best to launch you forward. It's incremental progress we seek here, and each progression will be a signal to your brain that you're advancing and that will give you hope and breed a healthy and vibrant optimism.

Every day in every way I think better and better thoughts.

Every day in every way, Dan, you think better and better thoughts.

Every day in every way Dan thinks better and better thoughts.

When your thinking reflects empowering thoughts day in and day out accomplishing your goals becomes much, much easier. You'll find you're less distracted as your focus sharpens. It may start with small projects and tasks but it will be evident. And as you grow this power will show as you ascend to greater things.

I am a genius applying my wisdom to making my dreams come true more exquisitely than I ever imagined.

Dan, you are a genius applying your wisdom to making your dreams come true more exquisitely than you could ever imagine.

Dan Wedin is a genius applying his wisdom to making his dreams come true more exquisitely than he could ever imagine.

The future will soon be a thing of the past, the late, great George Carlin quipped, and he's right. Tempus fugit. "Time flies" in Latin and no more truthful two words were ever coupled. The present will also soon be a thing of the past. Today is tomorrow's preview. *Think* today as you would *be* tomorrow. The good thinking habits you cultivate today will make you happier tomorrow just as the bad habits you allow yourself to think today you will pay for tomorrow.

Stopping bad thinking is much easier if you simply supplant them now with good thoughts and good affirmations. If the word *"aff"* or *"affirmation"* isn't the right word for you, use any you like. Mantra, saying, incantation, thought, lines; it doesn't really matter. The magic is in the repetition, the habitual use, and the good feelings they engender.

The past is prologue to the future, though, and do you want to continue at your current pace in pursuit of your goals and dreams? Or do you want to seize the day, fully inhabit this moment and watch as the outward circumstances of your life transform as you take charge of your thoughts and change them?

Again, every thought you think changes you in some small fashion. So why not intelligently direct the power of your thoughts to make change constant, and make that change for the better?

Between your ears lies the greatest computer on planet earth, to which I've alluded. Don't believe it? Right now it's processing this writing while hearing what's going on in the room, being aware of the temperature of the air, the comfort of your chair and attendant aromas in the room you currently occupy. All while thinking about sex. Or a snack. Or your next meal. Or maybe your last meal that's left you pleasantly or not so pleasantly full.

Do you want to achieve your goals, realize your dreams, and watch in wonder as your visions come to life? Do you want to be able to magically predict your future? Then, as **Alan Kay** of Xerox said, invent it. The exact quote:

"The best way to predict the future is to invent it."

Of course you can listen to that voice in your head that says *"quit"*. Are you a quitter? Few will admit it. But if your record is one of quitting and you're not proud of that, try this daily until all the quit is crowded out of your brain by better thinking:

I am a genius, applying my wisdom to my power of persistence.

Dan, you are a genius, applying your wisdom to your power of persistence.

Dan Wedin is a genius applying his wisdom to his power of persistence.

I am a genius applying my wisdom to creative persistence.

Dan, you are a genius applying your wisdom to creative persistence.

Dan Wedin is a genius applying his wisdom to creative persistence.

Every day in every way I demonstrate my admirable persistence.

Every day in every way, Dan, you demonstrate your admirable persistence.

Every day in every way Dan Wedin demonstrates his powerful and admirable persistence.

Okay, I tweaked the last line as it just felt good to add that word. Why not? Don't feel like there are rules here and go with your inspiration every time. You may find yourself down a rabbit hole but you'll never know it's that without trying something new. There are treasures to be found down some of those unexplored nooks and crannies. And don't just read these lines, remember to insert your name in the appropriate places where mine currently sits.

Fear not the new, break out of your mental "comfort zone" and change the way you think and you'll change the way you act and what your world looks like and feels like. Your reality is only based on your perception of that reality. And changing how you perceive something can be a very liberating exercise. It's not where you are, remember? It's the state you're in. Change the state of affairs upstairs and the entire palace takes on a new, liberating and often exhilarating character. When greater happiness and contentment is what you desire? Why not? You deserve it. You always have.

Fear of change is a curious thing. Often we know we need to change but we're mired in fear as even though we're not happy with where we are, it's familiar and in that way it's comfortable. Perhaps the most egregious example of this phenomenon is found in the "Battered Woman Syndrome". Long term abuse produces a sense of what's called "learned helplessness" making change next to impossible. And not taking action in some cases amounts to self-abuse, as in the "oppressed is as guilty as the oppressor" thought.

If you're being abused get help now by calling the National Domestic Violence Hotline at 1-800-799-7233. Please don't wait, you don't deserve abuse from anyone, anytime. Please call the Hotline now.

It's very easy for me to encourage you, *"Embrace change!"* But for some this simple suggestion may fall on deaf ears. Google "change process" and you'll be rewarded with a fabulous and voluminous array of sites describing various methods and practices. It's worthwhile to explore a few of these and prepare your mind for improvement. But let's say you don't want to do that and that's okay. Let's look at one common path.

Virginia Tech's Professional Continuing Education describes the transtheoretical model's five stages of change as precontemplation, contemplation, preparation, action and maintenance. So you begin in your current state, then move to considering changing, something we all do frequently and it ends there most of the time.

Then you pick up a book, are inspired by a TED Talk or an article or a conversation. Inspired by this new information and how contemplating it made you feel, you're moved to action. Now you've changed, but the vestiges of how you used to be remain. You're on the bubble of a relapse, a return to your previous thought patterns and behavior and you face a decision. Drop the change, or recommit yourself to this change which you view as an improvement.

You stick with it, hopefully, and over time the old patterns grow faint and lose their power. At a certain point returning to the old behavior becomes unthinkable as new thinking brings new perspectives, new powers and confidence. Confidence that with this thought-allied-with-action template you can now change a lot of behavior and move forward.

And let's face it, if you're going to awaken the mental giant within you're going to want to believe in yourself. You're going to want to believe in the concepts present in your ongoing internal conversation. And at first that may be a challenge. But that's okay. Just begin and let the lines flow. Your thoughts are connected to your actions and you'll notice yourself changing how you do things first in small ways. This, allowed to flourish by continued good thinking, will blossom into more profound, effortless actions as you proceed.

It's okay, as remember? Every thought you think changes you. So the more you repeat your I-You-She/He sequences the more believable it will become. Strive for sincerity, strive for focus. Say it internally, say it aloud, hell, shout it if you're feeling like shouting. That's probably best done in private! And always, always speak to yourself as if you are your own Best Friend. Do you struggle with that idea? Let's go over this important work again.

Pick up a copy of *"How to Be Your Own Best Friend"* on amazon.com. I just checked and found a used hardcover for $1.99. This short but beautiful book was written by Mildred Newman and Bernard Berkowitz, married-to-each-other psychoanalysts, as I've noted. Try to locate as recent a copy as possible. I have a first edition and the authors state some very outdated views on gay therapy. Times change, people change. But it takes no time to read and you'll want to return to it again and again as it will make you feel good. Why is that important?

When you feel good your brain runs on good chemistry and your body just works better. You think clearer with more focus. You're more optimistic which means you're more likely to have faith in whatever endeavor you choose. And by reading HTBYOBF more than once, you'll soon find that the resulting mindset can become your permanent happy self. Blissful self. Less-stressed self. And really, who doesn't want to be at their best more often, and with greater intensity? After all, you deserve it, don't you?

Good thinking's no secret

It takes so little time

Just think one good thought

One good thought at a time.

In time you'll find that certain things will spark thought patterns you've established and it will all happen automatically. In my case, as I said, when I begin a walk I'll often launch into "Every day in every way I get better and better..." It just happens. It regulates my thoughts, moods and actions.

It enables me to consciously (and automatically) check my stride and posture as I walk to maximize the health benefits of walking properly. I've researched this a bit and, as in most things, there's a right way, wrong way and relative to your habits, a better way. I seek the better way and constant improvement. You can, too. Constant improvement is exciting and heartening.

With practice you'll find your thoughts begin to assume an automatic nature indicating you're now on "Thought-Auto-Pilot" and programmed to think enlightening and empowering ideas and feelings through the endless power of auto-suggestion.

But make no mistake, while we're all different it is very likely that the majority of your thoughts will be elsewhere driven by the font of thought loops and random musings for which our left brains are well known. Yet just as the late Margaret Mead, famed anthropologist, noted about revolutions, they only take a small, committed minority of the population to foment. Think of your affs as this revolutionary force at work to change the way you think for the better.

We are what we think. All that we are arises with our thoughts. With our thoughts we make the world.

Buddha

"Your life is what your thoughts make it."

"It does not matter how slowly you go as long as you do not stop."

Confucious

Augment your reality with You Are A Genius. Then make it virtual, envision your ideal and then inhabit that world until you're living that reality. Control your thoughts, even in small increments and you'll be on the journey of constant self-improvement. Every thought you think changes your world, if only ever so slightly, remember? But change occurs in stops and starts and sometimes great leaps forward. Change the way you think, change the way you feel and you'll change the outward circumstances of your life in profound ways.

And an interesting thing happens as you progress. What's challenging today will be different tomorrow. The obstacles you may perceive at this moment will potentially vanish to be replaced by new ones. Yet as obstacle after obstacle is overcome that habit of relentless success over what's in your way feeds on itself. Soon obstacles will be things to be welcomed, recognized and overcome.

Now think back a bit, how many times in your life has a daunting challenge lay before you? And yet once you overcame it, got past it, looking over your shoulder you realized it was not nearly as daunting as it appeared. What looked like ferocious tigers were in fact paper tigers and you punched right through them.

It's all about being better than you were. You need compete with no one except who you were yesterday. It's a challenge, no question, yet one you can make your best habit. And the payoff can be enormous. Once you've committed your thoughts to this course of action it becomes second nature, and you'll find these empowering lines flowing through your consciousness. You'll revel in the growing understanding you'll gain of the power you'll personally wield as you focus your energies on your true goals and dreams. And once focused?

You'll find each day an exciting adventure as you ask, "How good can I make my day? How far can I go? And what will my life look like when I achieve my true potential?"

It's not where you are, it's the state you're in, my friend, as I've said. Repeatedly. Change your state of mind and you literally change where you are. And if you choose the right thoughts you can find yourself in a state of peace, of love, of understanding, of gratitude, of empathy and of happiness. Exchange the dreary for the cheery. After all, if you're having fun your joy will be contagious and if it spreads? Gosh, the world might end up a better place and that's all to the good, isn't it? And the world needs you at your best, in so many ways.

The Story We Tell Ourselves, About Ourselves

We are all storytellers, aren't we? It's how we were raised, it's how we entertain each other, it's how we make sense of what of the world we know. And we don't always get it right, and this includes the most powerful story of our life, the one we tell ourselves about ourselves.

Let's assume that this *"story"* is an unfinished work. That's plausible, isn't it? So this story we tell ourselves dictates how we feel and act, after all, this is who we are, right? Then by aligning that story with greater optimism, a more positive attitude, at this point your *"story"* begins to take on a new character. One imbued with honesty, realism, acceptance and forgiveness. And also pride, if that's what it takes. Give yourself credit where credit is due.

The story you tell yourself about yourself is a very powerful thing. What if we consciously shaped that story around our potential, our belief in ourselves, our ability to grow, our ability to succeed, our ability to secure happiness and prosperity, that would be a good thing, right? I certainly think it would. And if it resulted in greater self esteem, so be it. Bask in it. And in the sense that going forward you will always be your own best friend.

Change the way we look at something and it takes on a new character. We are often plagued with incomplete information not unlike a developing news story changes as new facts and perspectives emerge. This is why history is never quite completely set. It's an organic, changing and growing thing. And that includes yours.

A number of years ago I was travelling on business, working with struggling airlines to help them secure the media presence they needed to communicate with customers, especially new customers, and compete with the majors.

I was training a new salesman who was older than I was and I could sense that he wasn't comfortable with working for someone younger. Not an unusual phenomenon and one for which I had empathy. We had traveled to Ft. Lauderdale to meet with a foreign airline that seemed to be a good prospect.

In the limited pool of airlines in the world it's important to speak to the entire community to let them know we could be of service. And it's good to be a known commodity as the cast of players in the industry's highly mobile. Who you speak with today at airline "A" could be with airline "B" next week. Or with the next big startup.

Anyway, I was excited to be in Florida, I found Ft. Lauderdale charming, and we were staying at a lovely oceanfront property whose entrance faced town and whose ocean side contained a "Pusser's" (British bastardization of "Purser's, the ship's finance officer), a great waterfront restaurant and lounge with a fascinating raw bar. The array of unusual seafood on ice excited this son of Seattle and the west coast so I was happy to be there.

My new salesman? He was grumpy, testy and short with me. I invited him to Pusser's but he declined. On the way to the big meeting with the airline he called my room from downstairs and barked, *Meet me in the lobby!* I paused and told him calmly I would be down shortly.

When I exited the elevator it took two seconds to see his brow was furrowed, his lips turned down and impatience was all over his body language. I walked to him directly and never took my stare from his, though I worked to keep my countenance neutral. I'd studied a bit about body language and negotiation and was going to fix this then and there before we let it spill over into our meeting.

What was that call about?

I was tired of waiting for you!

Then why don't you change your flight and head back home because I'm your boss and you're so far out of line that I'm considering firing you right here, right now.

Now listen, mate, (he was of Irish descent and origin)...

No. I'm not going to listen. We agreed last night to meet at 8a. You're either going to accept that you work for me here or you won't be. I've discussed this with the owner and he's in full agreement.

This caused the guy to raise his eyebrows. We both knew he needed the job, he had been hired after begging the owner whose wife had been dead set against it. He knew he was in a spot and he could only get out of it by acquiescing.

I-I-I'm sorry.

Okay, but let that be the last of it. You may not be having any fun but frankly I enjoy Ft. Lauderdale, I had a great night, and I will not let you ruin my trip or this important visit I've been working on for three months, got it?

Glumly, he accepted.

Did his attitude change? No. He just internalized it. He was useless at the meeting as his demeanor was negative and his faux charm unconvincing and he really hadn't mastered how to explain what we did and how we did it. After all, he had a great reluctance when it came to asking questions about how our business worked. Rather than seeing it as professional curiosity, perhaps he viewed it as a sign of weakness. I had to intervene and take care of pushing it through. If your true feelings don't match your actions you're out of sync and whoever you're dealing with knows this on a subconscious or even conscious level. At a certain level of human endeavor you just can't fool people.

So I took note of the prospect's assessment of my employee's performance. It was painful. He was terrible for our brand as we were the friendly, smart group that could rescue a diminished ad budget with a highly creative method for gaining advertising without expending cash by leveraging unused inventory.

Genius system, really, that our owner had engineered. But it involved access to the airline's online reservation system, a major hurdle, and had to be handled articulately and with sensitivity. He exhibited neither and when challenged displayed a hint of hostility that was completely counterproductive. He had experience in the airline business but not in this end of it but since he "knew it all" he was a difficult student to guide through the maze.

We parted company following the visit and he returned to Palm Springs and me to Portland. He was let go soon after by consensus and of course, threw a giant tantrum and tried to threaten me physically at a "final check" airport meeting in Palm Springs which was pathetic. He finally signed the separation agreement which was the condition required for getting his separation check.

Had his attitude changed he could have enjoyed a much longer career with us but he was stuck in the role as his own worst enemy. A clear example of that deadly combo of arrogance and ignorance which always presages a disaster of some proportion for anyone allowing themselves to drift into the jaws of that vice.

I joked to the rest of the company that he'd told me, "I don't hate you Danny, just yer guts," in an Irish brogue. They knew I was kidding but the reality was he hated himself, where he found himself at age sixty, and other more personal elements in his story. He inspired me to write a line in my trip report and it's stuck with me as I've seen it play out repeatedly:

It's not where you are! It's the state you're in.

I know, Department of Redundancy Department memo. Again. But it bears repeating. Your attitude, not your image, is everything. Change your attitude and your image and your performance magically transforms. If the adage that one needs to tell a child something six times before they get it is true, how many times does an adult need to be told? And what if you selected a thought you definitely wanted to not just *"get"* but incorporate into the very essence of your being? How many repetitions would you be willing to perform to make that happen?

Do not, under any circumstances, be that person, the rigid victim of their own thoughts. And if the story sounds some familiar notes, begin today to supplant those negative emotions, ones you perhaps are sharing with the world around you. You can only try to hide this kind of internal reality, after all. Take action with a series of affs and thoughts that will begin the process of drowning out the negative, the masochistic, and the poisonous thoughts afflicting you. Auto-suggestion is your lifeboat away from those sinking feelings.

In short, begin the uplifting and highly enjoyable journey to becoming your own best friend. To give it a launching pad, pick up that copy of "How To Be Your Own Best Friend", the brilliant and short read that you may return to again and again. You have nothing to lose and perhaps you'll gain a friend or become an ever better friend to yourself. And self directed change occurs so much easier when you're in the right frame of mind.

The late Nora Ephron, noted journalist and filmmaker, related that she couldn't live without that book. For some it's a game changer and if the game needs changing buy it and read it. It is a jolt to the brain, a positive one, particularly when you're mired in self-defeating thinking that, naturally, leads to self-defeating behavior.

"Don't fight forces, use them."

Richard Buckminster Fuller (1895-1983)

Now let's say you're prone to a lack of ambition. Perhaps somewhere in your brain via childhood memories or things you heard said about you or your performance left a strong impression, though perhaps an unconscious one, that you would never really succeed in achieving your dreams. So what do you do?

There are numerous examples in the book, "Money is My Friend" of people who avoid making more money than their mother or father made. In fact, they'll sabotage their success to stay within an income level they feel is acceptable instead of simply maximizing their income.

So develop some new habits of thinking. They'll be your friends in achieving your ends. Unless you're perfectly happy with how you think now, in which case you might consider setting this book aside for another time or sharing it with another. Moving ahead means acknowledging that you'd like to change, to improve, to get better than you are at this moment. So if you're completely happy and satisfied this may not be for you.

However, if you do want to get better every day in every way, forge ahead. Embrace change, that ever-present force for better or worse and begin. Once you get started it just gets easier and easier. And more enjoyable. If you want more laughs in your life and yes, laughter may not be the best medicine but it's certainly right up there, try this:

I am a genius applying my wisdom to my sense of humor.

Dan, you are a genius applying your wisdom to your sense of humor.

Dan Wedin is a genius applying his wisdom to his sense of humor.

Keep in mind that your sense of humor is not just your ability to come up with a clever quip at the right moment. It's also your ability to see the humor in life, in what you think at times, and the outrageous behavior that some days surrounds all of us. A good belly laugh inspires excellent brain chemistry so seek those opportunities. A laugh a day is not enough. Laugh all you can, store them up. You'll need them. That's life.

And to close out this chapter on making habit-driven thinking your ally, try this:

I am a genius applying my wisdom to developing powerful thinking habits.

Dan, you are a genius applying your wisdom to developing powerful thinking habits.

Dan Wedin is a genius applying his wisdom to developing powerful thinking habits.

And then every day in every way you'll be thinking more and more empowering thoughts. That could change your life. It's changed mine. And I'm a lazy guy dedicated to having fun. In fact, my resume states my career goal is to *"Get paid for enjoying myself"* and has for years. Though I've rarely had to use it. So if I can do this and benefit tremendously I have high, high hopes for you.

What you'll end up doing is train your brain to just fly the plane while you go about seeking true balance and enjoying your daily life. The difference will be apparent as in the background, in your subconscious, will be thought loops, blazed neural pathways alive with affs that elevate your daily life and everything you do. If you stick with the *"You Are A Genius"* formula, in a few short weeks this will take place and these elevating affs will keep you experiencing improvements, enhancements and forward progress in your life.

Think of your practice with *"You Are A Genius"* concepts as James Allen taught us that *"Deeds are seeds and the harvest will appear in due season."* For thoughts are indeed seeds and most assuredly those planted seeds, nurtured with repetition and the known power of auto-suggestion will sprout, grow and bear fruit in the rich earth of your mind and the grand garden of your life.

There will no doubt be many who will master this, expand on this, refine this in ways beyond my humble talents. I applaud that enthusiastically. When it comes to human thinking we are all standing on the shoulders of giants. I'm just saying don't just stand there, listen to their potent thoughts. They're still trying to teach us, gone though they may be, as their wonderful conclusions live on. To good thoughts!

And somewhere out there is a person who will read this and throw themselves into it with ferocious enthusiasm. They will think empowering thoughts every day in every way. They will elevate their game and their performance and perhaps custom fit these mantras to their unique circumstances. I wish I could be there charting their progress as they take control of their very existence courageously empowering themselves with ever more relevant and exciting thinking.

And they may change the world! And this old world's never been more in need of empowered agents of change fighting for truth, justice and a better way. *Go Super Human!*

You. Can. Do. This. One thing that really matters in life is what you decide to do next. Make your next thought, your next move your best move. Begin that journey to a better, stronger, more successful You. *Why not?*

You Are A GENIUS

It's not where you are, it's the state you're in.

Chapter Five
Goals and Dreams
Versus Wishes and Hopes

Definitions:

Wish: feel or express a strong desire or hope for something that is not easily attainable; want something that cannot or probably will not happen.

Hope: a feeling of expectation and desire for a certain thing to happen.

Dream: a cherished aspiration, ambition, or ideal.

Goal: the object of a person's ambition or effort; an aim or desired result.

From Oxford Dictionary

Note that the word "ambition" is found in the definition of both goals and dreams. That's telling, isn't it? We've all known times in our lives when we lacked ambition, haven't we? And times when we've seen the results of our ambitions bear fruit. If you lack ambition, try this before proceeding:

I am a genius, applying my wisdom to my ambition.

Dan, you are a genius applying your wisdom to your ambition.

Dan Wedin is a genius applying his wisdom to his ambition.

Every day in every way my ambition grows.

Every day in every way, Dan, your ambition grows.

Every day in every way Dan Wedin's ambition grows.

We all have our wishes and hopes and goals and dreams, don't we? And for many they do not speak of the most important ones as they may feel it'll set them up for embarrassment. On top of the personal disappointment that comes from failing to reach an objective. Perhaps, as they do in debate, we should *"define terms"*.

If the desire is within your control shouldn't that logically be moved from the Wish list to the Goals column? Let's say your dream is to lay out and plant an English garden in your backyard. Or even just buy planter boxes for that herb garden you've dreamed of for your balcony. You want to achieve this. You want to see your dream become a reality. It's your goal, after all, right?

But is it really a goal if you've yet to begin to achieve it? No, it's not a goal, it's a wish, something you hope for. Of course this is just semantics, but perhaps an important distinction. Let's take that dream, that vision, that beautiful hope and transform it into a goal:

I am a genius, applying my wisdom to making a back deck herb garden to do list.

Dan, you are a genius applying your wisdom to making a back deck herb garden to do list.

Dan Wedin is a genius applying his wisdom to making a back deck herb garden to do list.

I actually did, for years, wish to have fresh herbs growing on our back deck that we could use in cooking. We're not talking about any big vision here. Years went by, and I wished on. Then I started saying the above. And within a day I wrote out a to do list. Somewhere deep in my brain I felt, rather than heard, a thought that okay, I'll make this list but I still don't have to do anything. That's the unconscious *"Lazy Dan"* protecting his indolent turf, a product of my *"Lizard Brain"*, felt rather than stated in words.

So I proceeded to write a list of the herbs we thought most desirable. It's a small deck so I kept it to five. A day or two later I was getting out of my car in the garage and stopped in my tracks and stared at a chromed étagère in the corner I'd been trying to get rid of. I'd even put it on craigslist to no avail. I once sold my wife's jewelry armoire for her and offered the étagère free to the buyer. She didn't want it, making it all the less desirable to me.

But now I saw this thing in a brand new light. See, it's not what we're looking at it's how we're viewing what we're looking at. It's not where we are, it's the state we're in, right? I had begun the process of moving a wish to a goal, and things were slowly changing.

The polished chrome étagère had five levels. That shocked me. I had five herbs on the list. The shelves were metal slats with one a punched-hole box of sorts, suitable for drainage.

I was a bit transfixed. Cozy back patio? One foot square footprint on the étagère. Had my subconscious seen this and begun the process of making that wish a tangible goal without any conscious thought on my part? I don't know. I don't care. All I know is that as soon as I had said the affirmations a few times things started to happen. Tangible things.

I moved the étagère to the deck. I cleaned it completely of all dust and dirt. It looked brand new and I'm not sure a more perfect unit could be chosen for this project. I bought the plants. Put them on the shelf. In the ensuing few days I bought more dirt, attractive blue ceramic planters, then transplanted the herb plants. Day by day the Herb Tower from Heaven took shape. A small example of setting your course to achieve a goal, and arriving at a destination.

It would be easy to doubt the source of my motivation, I know, but I've seen this play out in my life repeatedly. I'll find myself just unconsciously doing something without forethought that's connected with my affs. As James Allen notes in *"As A Man Thinketh"* all of the circumstances of your life are intimately connected to your thoughts. And I would add that this is true, even if you're unable to connect the dots clearly. And when I began using an aff to accomplish this goal I had no intention of relating it in my writing.

Yet now the herb tower is flourishing and serves as a reminder that if wishes are worthy, turn them into tangible goals. Make a goal, repeat the appropriate affs, make a list, and repeat the appropriate affs again. I'm sitting in the sun working on my laptop next to the herb tower as I write this.

The Rosemary on top is reaching for the blue skies. The Thai Basil's lush and wonderful. The Chive thrives. The Parsley's reaching out for more sun. And the Greek Oregano's preparing for its audition in a fabulous recipe I managed to extract from a Greek-American gentleman who used to run a deli. My goal is to make it, and share it. I can taste it. No joy in life like serving others.

Okay, this is a small goal, a very realizable one. But something I felt was of value yet it just sat there, unrealized. Is it a metaphor for a higher purpose, a grander dream? You'll have to be the judge and I encourage you to look inward for those dreams that you can bring to fruition with a few apropos affs to trigger action. Thought + Action = Results. Act is the blossom of thought, after all, isn't it?

And it's valuable to spend some time saying silently or out loud affirmations with global implications for your entire existence. Not tied to anything specific other than constant growth and improvement.

Every day in every way my LIFE is getting better and better.

Dan, every day in every way your LIFE is getting better and better.

Every day in every way Dan Wedin's LIFE is getting better and better.

Some dreams are perhaps better left as visions. Impossible visions but pleasant to contemplate, right? Be careful what you wish for, you might get it, right? Then again, as we discussed in Chapter Two, what is it that you truly want? Perhaps it's time to separate the dreams and wishes into two lists. How about *"Worthwhile Dreams"* and *"Pipe Dreams"*.

Write down both lists and look at them. Do you have them under the right heading? If you have doubts move any you're unsure of from *"Pipe Dreams"* to *"Worthwhile Dreams"*. We are creatures equipped with a huge, relatively speaking, capacity for vision, inspiration and perseverance so do not sell yourself short. Do not fear thinking big and dealing with the hulk that lies behind it, *fear of failure.*

Fear of failure is the enemy. It denotes an aversion to risk, which is a natural defense mechanism. So imagine this dream of yours is something you've decided to accomplish. It's a challenge as you imagine the steps necessary to achieve it in all its glory.

If you break it down into a step-by-step list, what happens? You begin to see the major undertaking as components, and if you truly break it down this way it's possible that this *"pipe dream"* is now just a series of *"worthwhile dream components"* that, with focused thought and effort, are eminently doable. And one by one as each smaller project is accomplished the dream becomes not just possible but inevitable.

When we view a dream in its entirety it can appear a complicated undertaking with endless hurdles, paths, questions and outcomes. One doesn't enter a *"Dream Academy"* and receive a course description with all of the classes and seminars and books to be absorbed listed. Quite the contrary, this is a self-directed effort, an autodidactic undertaking and the tendency is to look at the goal in total, as a single entity.

Yet wouldn't it be better to break it down, step by step, in chronological order? I like to cook and received early instruction from my Mother. Then I spent my last three years in high school on the Washington coast after beginning in Seattle. I took *"Seamanship & Boat Handling"*, and the accompanying course to complete the year was *"Bachelor's Home Ec"*.

The simple recipe layout to cook something's instructive. It's essentially a dream in microcosm. You're given a list of ingredients, tools and pans needed, the order in which they're assembled, temperature settings, timing and finishing techniques. And often plating instructions. I don't know about you but I have occasionally crafted a *"Dream on a Plate"* and looking at it is an amazing exercise when one considers all of the factors including chemistry, physics, the Maillard Effect and artistry. And every dish tells a story, doesn't it?

So consider putting together the recipe for your *Worthwhile Dreams*. Then take it calmly, with purpose, one step at a time. And when I'm cooking something I've made before I'm always questioning how and why things are done as I know in almost all cases there can be a better way. A cursory study of recipes for the same dish will reveal that food preparation, as in so many others things, is an arena where constant improvement is applauded and recognized.

Once you're clearly in touch with your dream, convert it to a goal by breaking it down into a series of projects that you can achieve one by one with each bringing you closer to realization. And if your dream is to create a lifestyle, great. Picture it in great detail, revel in it, imagine it in full living color and how you'll feel once you've created it and are actually living and breathing it.

If it's simply to gain something, be certain you develop a list of goals after assessing whether it's a *"Worthwhile Dream"* or *"Pipe Dream"*. Work on lists for the worthwhile dreams and forget the pipe dreams.

Unless the pipe dream's able to make that leap due to a gain in knowledge or confidence or other factor, ignore it. But don't let them float around your head. Wishing for things is not nearly as satisfying as working for things. In fact it can be quite a negative, unsatisfying practice. Why?

Wishing, frankly, is a waste of time. Perhaps it's a habit developed in childhood when wishes were magical things and sometimes situations *"Aladdinized"* and they came true due to the intervention of adults in our lives. But incessant wishing for something is thought unallied with action and that course rarely brings you to your destination. So learn the definitive difference between wishing and planning and discourage the wishing. This might help:

I am a genius, applying my wisdom to the achievement of my true goals.

Dan, you are a genius applying your wisdom to your true goals.

Dan Wedin is a genius applying his wisdom to his true goals.

Every day in every way I work to achieve my goals.

Every day in every way Dan, you work to achieve your goals.

Every day in every way Dan Wedin works to achieve his goals.

I am genius, applying my wisdom to making my dreams come true more exquisitely than I ever imagined.

Dan, you are a genius applying your wisdom to making your dreams come true more exquisitely than you ever imagined.

Dan Wedin is a genius applying his wisdom to making his dreams come true more exquisitely than he ever imagined.

I am a genius applying my laser-focused wisdom to the realization of my dreams.

Dan, you are a genius applying your laser-focused wisdom to the realization of your dreams.

Dan Wedin is a genius applying his laser-focused wisdom to the realization of his dreams.

Every day in every way I am getting better and better at auto-suggestion.

Every day in every way, Dan, you are getting better and better at auto-suggestion.

Every day in every way Dan Wedin is getting better and better at auto-suggestion.

And here's a powerful thought from the late Phil Laut:

I have enough time, energy, wisdom and money to achieve all of my desires.

Dan, you have enough time, energy, wisdom and money to achieve all of your desires.

Dan Wedin has enough time, energy, wisdom and money to achieve all of his desires.

Once you begin this journey of thought allied with purpose in the pursuit of a goal in pursuit of a dream, I suggest you consider the importance of maintaining focus. And since the to-do list that's exceedingly long can find you mired in the sheer length of the list, laser-guide your attention on one worthwhile goal at a time. Create a long term list of these goals so that once one is accomplished you don't skip a beat in your pursuit of the next. But do celebrate each achievement, and revel in the encouraging brain chemistry it inspires.

There's an old Russian Proverb with a bit of timely wisdom:

"If you chase two rabbits, you will not catch either one."

Indeed. Another fascinating angle to this concept is found in Tolstoy's short story, *"How Much Land Does a Man Need?"* Short story, yes, but one that stays with you forever. A great rubric on greed I highly recommend.

So you've set your goal, a component to reaching your dream. You're now possibly intent upon bringing this vision to your real world. That's exciting if you've made this commitment. And the more you centralize your thoughts and actions on this singular goal, the easier it will be to accomplish.

Ask yourself questions about this dream of yours and look not for immediate answers. Simply phrase the questions as intelligently as you possibly can and then do something else. Your subconscious will work on your question while your consciousness is absorbed by reading or playing or even sleeping.

And a good habit for a dream builder to cultivate is asking questions surrounding your goal just prior to turning in for the night. Moments of inspiration like the one I experienced in that Maui resort room are exciting and often true breakthroughs. You'll want to encourage this as challenges are much more easily overcome via inspired ideas and concepts. Why not use your brain power to greater effect?

Questions are just such powerful tools for accessing that broad and highly detailed storehouse of knowledge we've been accumulating throughout our lives, no matter your age. We read things, we hear things, we watch things and it's possible you know vastly more than your conscious life might reflect.

A couple of decades prior to this book's publication, a research team at Washington University's School of Medicine noticed that activity in a certain part of the brain was elevated when the research subject was at rest. They surmised that this was the brain's default mode so they named it the Default Mode Network.

This is the source of the answers that come to you when you're not focused on the problem, perhaps even while you're sleeping. This is a powerful source of our intuition, and solutions not produced by conscious thought. Tap into your sedubconscious by asking those intelligently phrased questions and then go for a walk. Get a coffee. Take a nap.

What you know you know is as important as what you know you do not know or perhaps what you know but can't instantly access a clear memory for. Exploring the vastness of your brain can be as easy as a simple question such as, *"What do I remember from blank?"* and blank can be a person, a year, a place, an experience.

Here's an expanded version of Goethe's quote:

"Until one is committed, there is hesitancy, the chance to draw back, always ineffectiveness. Concerning all acts of initiative and creation, there is one elementary truth the ignorance of which kills countless ideas and splendid plans: that the moment one definitely commits oneself, then providence moves too."

Johann Wolfgang von Goethe (1749-1832)

Yes, the moment one definitely commits oneself, then *"providence"* moves also, as I've noted. Goethe was referring to his deity, but I think there's a deeper truth here. When you completely commit to something, be it a business idea, a marriage, a project, whatever, then it seems the forces of the universe and in fact your fellow human beings seem to aid you in your quest. And never fear asking for help. We all like to help our fellow human beings, don't we?

But *"complete commitment"* is the key. If your commitment's on fire today and smoldering embers tomorrow on the verge of going out, then you're less than committed and more interested in just seeing the thing through, if at all. If it's not worth your full commitment, consider dropping it altogether. Half a commitment is at times worse than none at all.

Thoroughly vet what you truly want to do. Look at it from all angles. Imagine life with this thing done. Really imagine it, cloak it in garments, give it as much imaginative life as you can. And just ask yourself, point-blank. Is this really what I want to do? If the answer's unwaveringly

"Yes!"? Then go. Let's say you want to buy a lot at your favorite beach and build a long dreamt-of beach cabin. Try this:

I am a genius, applying my wisdom to building my dream beach cabin.

Dan, you are a genius, applying your wisdom to building your dream beach cabin.

Dan Wedin is a genius applying his wisdom to building his dream beach cabin.

Every day in every way I get better and better at building my beach cabin.

Every day in every way, Dan, you get better and better at building your beach cabin.

Every day in every way Dan Wedin gets better and better at building his beach cabin.

If you're facing financial challenges along the way, open your imagination to different and new ways of raising that capital.

I am a genius, applying my wisdom to allowing more money into my life than I could imagine before.

Dan, you are a genius applying your wisdom to allowing more money into your life than you could imagine before.

Dan Wedin is a genius applying his wisdom to allowing more money into his life than he could imagine before.

Every day in every way I grow more and more prosperous.

Every day in every way, Dan, you grow more and more prosperous.

Every day in every way Dan Wedin grows more and more prosperous.

Make building that beach cabin a centralizing purpose in your life, but not at the expense of the rest of it. So continue with your beach cabin-themed affs but continue also with your basics that help propel every area of your life to improvement mode and indirectly assist you in your stated goal. When your goal is constant improvement one single day of saying the affs with feeling a couple of dozen times can vault you forward. Now imagine the impact of three-hundred-sixty-five consecutive days of consistent movement forward.

Every day in every way I am getting better and better.

Every day in every way Dan you are getting better and better.

Every day in every way Dan Wedin is getting better and better.

I am a genius, applying my wisdom.

Dan, you are a genius applying your wisdom.

Dan Wedin is a genius applying his wisdom.

And remember, what you say is important. How you say it is even more important. One can write a very persuasive speech but delivered in a monotone voice with no emotion or variation and it falls flat. In fact, no one listens after a minute or two to your presentation as it's sucking the life force out of your audience. Cue the head down, looking at their phone note.

Speak with profound understanding, speak with joy, speak with emotion. Why not? If you're going to do it, do it with feeling, revel in your personal sense of joie de vivre. This is your life, these are your dreams and goals, and inherent throughout this journey is the underlying goal of setting you on a course of constant and real self-improvement. Enthusiasm is your fuel, your ally. And this is how you myelinate that neural pathway associated with this goal. That's the path to automatically inspiring those actions that will help you achieve success.

You're going to have thoughts streaming through your head throughout so why not capitalize on that existing flow and focus a portion of it on growing day in and day out? You will not regret it, regardless of how far you go. You will have made progress. And as the thought loops come back to you without conscious effort again and again you'll realize that your persistence is paying off.

Your life is happening anyway as time marches inexorably on. Instead of a semi-static state, why not use the power of your thoughts to give it wings and begin a journey with a great and worthwhile purpose? Commit yourself to making every day you're fortunate enough to be alive your masterpiece as, hey, this is your life and each precious day is really all you have for certain. And the day ain't over yet so don't assume a thing.

Does this mean every day from here on out will be a *"masterpiece"*? Highly unlikely. But it's what we're aspiring to here that counts. We want to elevate our game, it doesn't follow that every dart one throws is a bullseye. But over time the cluster of results tighten around that objective. That's the result, and getting better at producing those results every day in every way and being conscious of that is the key. So celebrate progress wherever you find it.

As I've noted, you're going to make more progress if you're in a good mood and if you're fervent in your desire to build that sparkling neural pathway. Guard your mental state against defeatism, fatigue and negative emotions. Try this one again and as often as you feel you need it. You're not going to live in blissful nirvana at all times, that's a fact, but what you can do is eliminate that ennui that robs you of the moderately blissful state that makes life much more enjoyable:

I am a genius applying my wisdom to my personal happiness.

Dan, you are a genius applying your wisdom to your personal happiness.

Dan Wedin is a genius applying his wisdom to his personal happiness.

If that doesn't strike a note that makes you smile? Try this:

I am a genius applying my wisdom to truly deserving personal happiness.

Dan, you are a genius applying your wisdom to truly deserving personal happiness.

Dan Wedin is a genius applying his wisdom to truly deserving personal happiness.

Every day in every way I grow happier and happier.

Every day in every way, Dan, you grow happier and happier.

Every day in every way Dan Wedin just grows happier and happier.

Over the course of my life I've known many people in professional and social and family situations. And a number have been less than happy, despite being wonderful people. Sometimes a lack of personal charm can make one feel more separated in a social situation than they should be. For those who feel that can be a challenge I suggest this. Don't laugh, I've seen this work:

I am a genius, applying my wisdom to my personal charm.

Dan Wedin

Dan, you are a genius applying your wisdom to your personal charm.

Dan Wedin is a genius applying his wisdom to his personal charm.

I am a genius, applying my wisdom to my sense of humor.

Dan, you are a genius applying your wisdom to your sense of humor.

Dan Wedin is a genius applying his wisdom to his sense of humor.

I am a genius applying my wisdom to my intense listening skills.

Dan, you are a genius applying your wisdom to your intense listening skills.

Dan Wedin is a genius applying his wisdom to his intense listening skills.

I am a genius applying my wisdom to my deep sense of personal confidence.

Dan, you are a genius applying your wisdom to your deep sense of personal confidence.

Dan Wedin is a genius applying his wisdom to his deep sense of personal confidence.

Is this going to make you instantly more popular? I don't know, as I don't have a sense of your personal motivation. But I already like you better knowing you're reading this book!

Yet imagine if you add some charm, listen carefully, are confident and have a sense of humor. I'm going to guess that yes, your popularity is going to be enhanced. After all, you deserve a life that just keeps getting better every day in every way, don't you?

Carrying negative baggage that's dragging you down? Sometimes this can be more of a bad mental habit than an inevitable burden. Once you are thinking less of the negative and more of the uplifting, the negative begins to fade and soon is simply a memory of something you've let go. You've made a conscious decision to defuse the negative thoughts and feelings that are inspiring unpleasant brain chemistry:

I am a genius applying my wisdom to letting things go.

Dan, you are a genius applying your wisdom to letting things go.

Dan Wedin is a genius applying his wisdom to letting things go.

I am a genius applying my wisdom to leaving the past behind.

Dan, you are a genius applying your wisdom to leaving the past behind.

Dan Wedin is a genius applying his wisdom to leaving the past behind.

You do not know how many days you have left. No one does. One of the true facts of life. So consider committing yourself to making the rest the very best. Why not? Who wants to be circling the drain, awaiting the inevitable? That day will come soon enough so don't waste your time contemplating the end. Embrace its inevitability, for sure, that's a motivating factor, but don't wallow in despair and dwell on it. Treat today as a new beginning and stock your consciousness with joyous, empowering and enlightening thinking.

Launch your own Great Enlightenment! It worked for humanity and it will work for you. Without the Enlightenment we wouldn't have had the French Revolution and while a lot of attention is paid to the excesses of that cultural upheaval, it's arguably the most important single event in Western Civilization. And the Founders of this nation studied the great thoughts and ideas in the compiled works known as *"Encyclopédie"*, a rich chronicle of Enlightenment thoughts and ideals. It was a crucial element in the great leaps forward the human race has made in governing, science, art and literature.

Take a moment and compile a list of those things bouncing around on the train of your thoughts and see how easy it is to separate the wishes and hopes from the goals and dreams. Focus on the realizable dream and then craft a list of goals that will help you begin, continue and finally realize that dream.

History is littered with wonderful biographies of those who seized that dream in their head and then set about bringing it to reality, achieving one goal after another. And overcoming one obstacle after another. Obstacles only appear daunting from one side, once you've brainstormed a list of how you're going to get past it most likely they will shrink considerably.

And once you're past it? You wonder why you were so concerned, possibly. Or you'll feel great pride in your ability to power your way through, around or over as you creatively put all of your skills to work. Think back and view the movie of your life. How many obstacles have you already overcome?

If you're anything like me you've made it past what seemed like daunting circumstances, like raging rapids with rocks and twists and turns and then suddenly? You're sailing along in smooth water looking back.

Fear not your obstacles, relish them. They serve as tests of your intelligence, your resolve and your ability to perhaps enjoy a stroke of, yes, genius. They happen, and they will happen to you. Simply program your brain to tap into the genius and wisdom you already possess. View the obstacle as an opportunity, a challenge to be met and overcome and in reality just another waypoint on your way to the success you envision. And when you do overcome it? Don't forget to celebrate that achievement!

Now I suggest you consider writing that list. Your beautiful dream is at stake. Don't let that dream, or yourself, down. Why not make a conscious decision right now to leverage the known power of auto-suggestion to upgrade the version of You residing in your subconscious?

It's there for the taking through the power of your own thoughts, every day in every way. As the journey of a thousand miles begins with a single step, your journey to Your Dream begins with a single thought. *Just Think It.*

You Are A GENIUS

It's not where you are, it's the state you're in.

Chapter Six
Auto-Suggestion;
Thought-Action-Results

Merriam-Webster defines Auto-Suggestion this way:

noun: auto-suggestion

the hypnotic or subconscious adoption of an idea that one has originated oneself, e.g. through repetition of verbal statements to oneself in order to change behavior.

That's relatively straightforward, isn't it? By repeating a good thought to yourself it becomes part of your subconscious, part of who you are and who you aspire to be.

Auto-Suggestion is a powerful force and has been employed since time immemorial in religion, advertising, the military, classrooms, parenting, mentoring and countless other settings. It's simply the practice of seeking mental progress through repetition of a thought designed to alter thought patterns. Auto-Suggestion is at its heart lines or affs that you choose and repeat to yourself until the repetition is transformed into habitual behavior.

When it comes to Suggestion, think, *"Eat your vegetables."* Your Mother ever utter that ad nauseam to you? It's likely. I remember hearing it from my Wife's late Father who at the time hadn't heard it from his Mother in over half a century. That's staying power. This is where the thought is passed down, incorporated and it changes behavior. Every day in every way. And by the way, he lived to be one hundred and one.

So it's obvious that Suggestion and Auto-Suggestion are powerful forces in our lives. They work. And again, as the late Bucky Fuller noted, *"Don't fight forces, use them."* This is a time-tested tool that one wants to employ for their benefit. But this is where *"choose wisely"* comes in.

You no doubt have a number of auto-suggestive phrases ensconced in your daily thoughts. They may be good, they may be bad, some are perhaps indifferent. What I suggest is you choose the thoughts, the affirmations that most speak to your current needs and conditions. We want to move your thinking processes, at whatever speed, toward thoughts and habits that supplant what's wrong, strengthen what's weak, and help you become a better, more empowered person. A more self-accepting person, and one capable of reaching their full potential in life, in love and for the rest of your days.

"You're a dumbshit!", I was told once. As a child it would have cut deep as it was a person I trusted and had known a long time. I'd delivered directions to this person and I'd gotten one turn wrong as we were new to the area. Cloverleafs can be slightly confusing at times.

But this was not delivered when I was a child. It didn't hurt my feelings, actually, I knew it wasn't true. What it did was display to me that this person was not their own best friend. And that if they'd call me that then this was highly likely part of their internal discourse with themselves. A sad example of a well-myelinated pathway that's a burden, not a benefit. We really don't treat others any better or worse than we treat ourselves as we all know. Or most of us, anyway.

But let's say this was barked in anger to a child who'd done something stupid. And let's say every time the child erred they heard this. Imagine the impact on their self-esteem, their self-worth and their overall attitude toward themselves. It's perhaps likely that they, too, might begin calling themselves a dumbshit, or something equally as damaging as that neural pathway was formed and myelin coated repeatedly. And when it converts to Auto-Suggestion this way it may take tremendous effort to dislodge the thought, to stop the habit. And that may never occur.

This is a classic demonstration of rudeness, of course, but it's damaging not just to the target but to the perpetrator themselves as insults hurled in anger give rise to feelings of guilt. And oddly, additional anger toward the insulted. When I raised the issue with this individual later their excuse was that I brought out the worst in them. Now that's a clever shifting of responsibility for a wrong.

So we know the power of auto-suggestion and it's used on you daily whether you like it or are conscious of it or not. So why not turn it into a powerful force for good in your own life? And if you are impatient or feel the need, explore hypnosis. What can it do for you?

When I was considerably younger I was a cigarette smoker. I loved the habit and I also included cigars and a pipe occasionally. And I greatly enjoyed rolling my own with Dewey Eggbert's "Drum" tobacco. I would call tobacco *"Sir Walter Raleigh's gift to the world"*, and tell people, *"I've succumbed to the blandishments of Lady Nicotine"*. Yeah, I had it bad; total nicotine addict.

I'd grown up with two smoking parents and it seemed everyone smoked in the movies. It was what you did when you grew up and when I was younger, like most children, I wanted to be older. So I smoked, starting at age eleven on the sly and really getting into it after I turned fifteen. Hanging around the fishing docks it was a near rite of passage.

I tried to quit once and made it for eight months saying I'd only smoke when having alcohol before succumbing to it once again while having a glass of milk. Go figure. Then I made a concerted effort to go cold turkey and made it thirteen months. One night at the dinner table my wife invited me to start smoking again. I was incredulous, but she said quitting had changed my personality and not for the better.

My two children at the time agreed so I sincerely apologized and immediately went to the store after dinner and bought a carton of cigarettes. I remember quite clearly the satisfaction I felt lining them up neatly in my "cigarette drawer". I was the happiest guy in town. I'd been a smoker who wasn't smoking, not a good combination. I gave up the idea of quitting at that point.

My logic was smoking was something I needed and adding months or years onto the end of my life, which from that vantage point appeared quite likely to be the least happy days of my tenure here, was pointless. I wanted happiness and congeniality and I wanted it now.

Then a couple of years later a friend from work was told by his physician that he needed to quit smoking. He tried. And tried again but confessed he just couldn't quit. So when a hypnotist ran an ad in the local paper with a screaming headline that said, "STOP SMOKING" for $29.95 I clipped it and showed it to him. You game? He was.

By the time the night rolled around I'd enlisted four other people at work who also wanted to quit. My friend and I went to the hotel early and hit the bar for drinks and a smoke or two; of course we chain-smoked. Anyway, we joined seven hundred other people and were taught the fundamentals of self-hypnosis. And I've since read that literally all hypnosis is, in fact, self-hypnosis. I'm not an expert on the subject so I don't know for sure but it sounds logical and it's oft-repeated by some who appear to have great experience in the art.

So we went through the hour and a half routine culminating with *"waking up"* feeling fantastic, on cue, to a room whose floor was covered with loose cigarettes and cigarette packs. The hypnotist had instructed us to throw them into the air at one liberating moment. We all left the hall, feeling great. I got in my car and drove home, though I was stuck in an I-5 construction jam that caused a half hour delay. Great time for a smoker to relax with a cigarette, right?

I had a pack in the side pocket of the driver's door and had an extra lighter in a center-of-the-dash compartment. Never once did I consider having a cigarette. When I got home I marched to my cigarette drawer, removed eight packs and deposited them in the trash can under the sink. My wife observed this and voiced her skepticism. But I persevered, basically on auto-pilot.

The next day at work I was a bit dazed and confused. After all, I was a heavy smoker and had really hit them hard the day of the event, finishing a Marlboro in the door of the hall to reach eighty-three. And then fifteen minutes in he gave us a smoke break. Rather humorously everyone immediately jumped at the chance for that last cig in a bit of a panic. Yet spirits were high and the level of expectation was as well.

Everyone on the deck I had chosen, in the sideways rain and wind on the mighty Columbia River, had one. I squeezed in two. Remember, I was doing this for a friend, a mercy mission, and perhaps didn't have a one hundred percent dedication to the final result. And what was that final result?

I quit. Completely. Never even thought about cigarettes and once at a party someone lit one and handed it to me. Laughing, I took one puff. And put it out. I was done. Years later I was heading up a *"Stop Smoking"* campaign at a company where I was general manager and offered anyone who quit a handsome financial reward if they could go one year without smoking. And I offered to buy them an e-cig kit to help them quit. Big mistake.

While testing it for a particularly heavy smoker who couldn't figure out how to use it, I took a puff. Like a stroke of magic I was instantly hooked, the thing looked like a cigarette and the well-myelinated pathway lit up as the nicotine coursed through my brain. But that's a different story.

My point is I went into the hypnosis session after having a couple of drinks, and having very little commitment to anything save my friend's health and it worked like a dream. That experience opened my eyes to the power of hypnosis but I'm not recommending it, just relating a story. It's a very personal decision. But I pondered the fact that a dramatic mental change had occurred via hypnosis. And it was fascinating to me that just the suggestion that we were going to wake up and *"feel great"* worked. I noted that.

And returning to *"Suggestible You"*, Vance notes that the myth that only the weak-minded can be hypnotized is dead wrong. There are those without the ability but it actually is a talent and this ability to focus comes into play in many areas of one's life to their great benefit.

I do think during the last couple of years I've entered a light state of hypnosis where my focus has been very deep and I felt a deep sense of relaxation and satisfaction. This has happened a number of times and these events seem to be sizable leaps forward for me. But what I'm recommending here is repetition and concentration. As you get better at focusing perhaps you'll experience a similar feeling. We're all different, yes, and we all have varying abilities to focus so seek your best techniques and explore hypnosis if that's of interest.

All of our thought patterns are different and we all respond to stimuli in a myriad of ways. Get to know how you respond, always a good thing in many pursuits in life. And as the Greeks taught us, *"Know thyself."* And it is your brain and your thoughts they're referring to here.

If you are curious about hypnosis I suggest great caution in selecting a practitioner. Get references, talk to your doctor and talk to patients who've been treated by the individual. And check with the Better Business Bureau. There are a number of illuminating clips on YouTube and a TED talk or two:

https://www.youtube.com/watch?v=RWMYNTnoEyQ

https://www.youtube.com/watch?v=CZQrz6A7fi4

Perhaps the most illuminating presentation I've seen on hypnosis:

https://www.youtube.com/watch?v=oZllg9-eBmk

What goes on in your subconscious is very powerful. And largely out of our control as we involuntarily breathe, blink, react to spiders, fear heights and so on. But through the power of auto-suggestion and conscious repetitive thought we can profoundly influence these reactions. Why do that?

Let's say you're a smoker and would like to be free of the habit. Let's say you have an eating disorder that leaves you consistently underweight or overweight. Or you're plagued with panic attacks that debilitate you to the point of paralysis. Or that some subconscious force keeps you from doing that which your conscious brain in logical fashion feels you can. Stage fright, anyone?

Against these afflictions sweeps in a conscious effort to seek help, to change, to be alleviated from the struggle and stress the condition creates in your life. And often the expense, as well.

If you commit yourself to constant improvement in all phases of your life, and you seek happiness just keep repeating to yourself your favorite aff of the moment. Before retiring, upon rising and throughout the day. The opportunities are endless. Why not?

In my experience when I'm motivated to change my mood, focus on a problem or position myself to get something done I'll often play with different approaches. Changing the words that are plugged into the basic aff can be quite interesting and help you center on the most effective approach. Get creative, use what you're trying to accomplish, where you want to mentally reposition yourself and just think it. Let the process of evolution occur and you'll soon land on an ideal or close to ideal line and you'll feel the effect.

If you find yourself in a bad mood try to articulate it to yourself and repeat an aff that counteracts it. You don't have to go from sad to glad in one line but by focusing on the positive element you wish to inspire you can move the mental dial.

I am a genius applying my wisdom to thinking happier thoughts.

Dan, you are a genius applying your wisdom to thinking happier thoughts.

Dan Wedin is a genius applying his wisdom to thinking happier thoughts.

Of course, if your sadness is based in a personal loss you're aware of then feeling sadness is a natural part of the healing process. Don't be in denial about emotions arising from legitimate causes. Those feelings will pass but in the moment just feel them. Ask yourself questions about those feelings. Know thyself, right? So in those cases just a solid and more general approach might be the best thing for you.

Every day in every way I'm getting better and better.

Every day in every way Dan, you're getting better and better.

Every day in every way Dan Wedin is getting better and better.

I like to start the day with my most commonly utilized aff and then take stock of what I need for that day and for that moment. You'll have "feelings" that will guide your choices but I've found it effective to start each day with that baseline. Though there have been times when an aff from the previous day is so powerfully attractive mentally that it just continues when I wake up. This is a powerful sequence so go with this flow. Try starting each day at first with:

Every day in every way I'm getting better and better.

Dan, every day in every way you're getting better and better.

Every day in every way Dan Wedin is getting better and better.

I am a genius applying my wisdom to getting better and better every day in every way.

Dan, you are a genius applying your wisdom to getting better and better every day in every way.

Dan Wedin is a genius applying his wisdom to getting better and better every day in every way.

110

It's not a straight path up so don't expect that. There may be exceptions but for the vast majority of us it will be, over time, a habit that can help you slowly, inexorably take control of your conscious and subconscious mind, seed it with fertile thoughts and change the way you feel and view your life. And the confidence you'll grow will hearten you, encourage you to push on, and enhance and strengthen these thoughts. Your outward circumstances will come to reflect this inner journey. Savor it, note the progress and continue the mental march onward and upward. You can do this.

And the beautiful thing about embarking on this journey is that day by day you'll feel different, the lines will flow, you'll adopt ones specific to your unique circumstances and moods. And as the neural pathways light up and are myelinated the ease with which the thoughts will flow may come to astound you. As you think so shall you become.

Now let's deal again with the idea of what you deserve. Your conscious brain may acknowledge that you deserve the best, that you deserve to be wealthy, prosperous, happy and successful. Does your subconscious brain share in this conscious belief? Who cares? Because who's in charge here, your vast subconscious and all of its Byzantine chambers, corridors and mirrored halls? The one that wakes you up in the middle of the night in a cold sweat with a troubled heart? Perhaps.

So let's open the door to that subconscious through consciously and carefully chosen thoughts and the power of auto-suggestion. Wouldn't you rather begin the process of changing the way you think consciously and slowly implanting in your subconscious empowering, beautiful thoughts? I'm guessing you would but there will be naysayers, will there not? Free country of 328 million minds, with 7 billion plus on the planet. There will be naysayers, yes indeed, and that's fine. We all get the choice to select our own path when it comes to what we decide to think.

But do we get to select our own future? I say we do. Imagine again your life as your favorite boat. If you're afraid of the water pick some other conveyance or focus on the garden of your mind or your mind as a computer. So imagine your "vessel" is being tossed upon the often turbulent seas of life. Subject to wind, waves, currents and the occasional floating obstacle. Where is this boat going? Would you like to find out?

I suggest you look at that boat, and focus on the wheelhouse or steering wheel depending on your vision. Is anyone at the wheel? This boat is your life, after all. Now envision you rising from your bunk or your comfortable chair in the salon and walking directly to that wheel. This is your station. Picture your destination! What does it look like, what does it smell like? Are there beaches? A beautiful city? An exotic tropical locale? Romance, perhaps?

Set your course for the ideal destination, i.e., your dream, that appeals to you the most. Now look ahead. Assume a good stance and put both hands on the wheel. Now that you know the destination, set the auto-pilot, which of course is your steady stream of empowering thoughts, and watch this ship begin to turn in the direction you want to go, the one you know you deserve. Stay steady, stay vigilant and affirm, reaffirm, and confirm. Every day in every way. Your chances of arrival at the sunny shore of your ideal, whatever form or shape that might take, has been greatly enhanced.

Use "every day in every way" as your constant companion. Your best friend, really. It will keep you moving ahead consistently. Or on course, if you will. And for those things that arise, those thoughts or feelings that do not honor you, that do not help your cause, that decay your spirit, try this:

I am a genius, applying my wisdom to being a richly deserving person.

Dan, you are a genius, applying your wisdom to being a richly deserving person.

Dan Wedin is a genius, applying his wisdom to being a richly deserving person.

Every day in every way I become a more deserving person.

Dan, every day in every way you become a more deserving person.

Every day in every way Dan Wedin becomes a more deserving person.

Why not encourage feelings of abundance in every area of your life? And if you feel you need more self-discipline, encourage an abundance of self-discipline with a strategic aff of your own creation, then use it liberally. Repeatedly. With passion and emotion. You'll be employing auto-suggestion to the slow turning of the *Good Ship You* and once in control you'll find the possibilities are endless.

Say these things as often as feelings of unworthiness come over you. When your self esteem ebbs. One of the ports of call along your journey shall be a warm, sunny and colorfully charming harbor you can return to again and again. And it's called self esteem. Without it your life can be a burden, and you can feel like a burden as you trudge through uninspired days and lonely nights.

Make a choice. And make this one not for the person you are right now, but the person you're becoming as you affirm your worth as a being on this planet, one that has as much right to be here as the mightiest king, the richest titan and holiest supplicant. It will be the difference between living life inspired, or dog-tired. Or just treading water, watching the ship of your dreams drift away. My wish for you is great inspiration, great happiness and great accomplishment.

You've got to think, it's part of life. So choose to think in a way that makes every day in every way better and better. Why not?

Now let's imagine for a moment you feel somewhat lost. You're not quite certain where to start here. I suggest you consider just launching into this enterprise with this:

Every day in every way I am getting better and better.

Every day in every way, Dan, you are getting better and better.

Every day in every way Dan Wedin is getting better and better.

How does that make you feel? Does it give you hope? Are you motivated to go on as you feel a bit of excitement? Hey, is there anyone out there who can honestly say they're completely finished improving, growing and gaining knowledge and wisdom?

I hope not, but in a country of 328 million; okay, there will be a group and that's fine. More power to them. Contentment is a soothing force and worth preserving. But I suggest you consider savoring contentment while never being quite satisfied. Save that for the finish.

Just keep saying those three lines over and over, whenever the opportunity presents itself. Of course, not when you should be listening to someone talking to you. Let's not start any bad habits. And pay close attention to how it sounds and if you can, say it out loud. Say it with confidence. Yell it a time or two. Say it with emotion and feeling. The more you mean it, the stronger the signal, the deeper it will penetrate and reverberate throughout your subconscious.

I related my habit to a friend once and he said,

"Oh, you're brainwashing yourself."

I snickered. And I asked him if saying a prayer was brainwashing oneself. If watching the same commercial repeatedly was allowing oneself to be brainwashed (*shaky ground, this argument!*). Then I explained that we're not attaching electrodes to our brain. We're not forcing some dogma on ourselves that conflicts with what we know to be true. We're simply acknowledging that as we think, so we become. And that we are the direct result of what we have thought and we will think, after all.

If you accept the concept Darwin espoused that the highest stage of our moral culture is when we learn to control our thoughts, it simply follows. And most of us, anyway, feel inside that yes, we do seek constant improvement. It's why we read, it's why we learn new things, it's why we exercise, it's why some of us go to church. After all, in the case of the latter if you're a believer not everyone's just ushered into heaven, right? It requires a certain level of moral behavior and not all of us were born automatically honest and pure. I know I wasn't.

I am a genius applying my wisdom to every thought I think.

Dan, you are a genius applying your wisdom to every thought you think.

Dan Wedin is a genius applying his wisdom to every thought he thinks.

When a negative thought/feeling clouds your brain, stop it in its tracks with a countering, empowering thought. But first take note of how this thought and mood affects your body language. Shoulders forward? Facial expression look or feel depressed? Feeling lethargic? Maybe it's a relationship riding a rough patch:

I am a genius applying my wisdom to my relationships.

Dan, you are a genius applying your wisdom to your relationships.

Dan Wedin is a genius applying his wisdom to his relationships.

I am a genius, applying my wisdom to my personal happiness.

Dan, you are a genius applying your wisdom to your personal happiness.

Dan Wedin is a genius applying his wisdom to his personal happiness.

I am a genius applying my wisdom to allowing more love into my life every day in every way.

Dan, you are a genius applying your wisdom to allowing more love into your life every day in every way.

Dan Wedin is a genius applying his wisdom to allowing more love into his life every day in every way.

And pay attention to the difference in the way you carry yourself while walking or your posture at rest when you're troubled. Then change your thoughts, and change your physical attitude. And stick with it and feel the difference. And don't underestimate the power of changing your body language first and letting your brain follow. There's tremendous evidence that this *"fake it until you feel it"* technique has great value and effect.

It's when you're in a less-than-stellar mood that it's most important to utilize *"You Are A Genius"* techniques. And don't allow yourself to get discouraged if you don't get instant results. This can leave you feeling even worse. Just persist until you begin to feel the power of automaticity and that will happen over time.

You deserve happiness and when regrets from the past or worries about your future dominate it can rob you of the joy and bliss of the present. And the present is the gift that just keeps on giving if you're in the right mood. Remember, it's not where you are, it's the state you're in so if you're in a sorry state, supplant it with something capable of moving you forward:

Every day in every way I am getting happier and happier.

Every day in every way, Dan, you are getting happier and happier.

Every day in every way Dan Wedin is getting happier and happier.

But if you consistently battle feelings that make you feel bad, discuss it with your doctor or naturopath. You could possibly have an underlying condition that could be helped with medicine or therapy. Do some research on the topic. Try taking a reputable daily vitamin with minerals from a solid brand. This has been shown to be helpful for some people. We're in a gifted age with brilliant science at our fingertips. Avail yourself of it.

So use Auto-Suggestion to your benefit and watch how it changes how you think, how you feel and the outcomes you enjoy. We are what we think so just make a mentally global decision that you're going to take part of that vast stream of thought and divert a portion of it for conversion to consciously repeated thoughts that help elevate you.

The tool is right here. Simply begin to forge the habit of living consciously, proactively, and with every intention of finding yourself getting better and better every day in every way. Your self-crafted future of powerful thinking awaits your arrival.

And the igniting sparks of empowering thinking will just keep myelinating your neural pathways beautifully. Just begin and let the power of beneficial behavior be your constant companion. Just keep in mind that you want to do this with intensity and purpose. Search for those affs that inspire, that excite and exhilarate you. You'll find yourself glad this habit's on board for the most exciting voyage of *Your Life*.

You Are A GENIUS

It's not where you are, it's the state you're in.

Chapter Seven
Thought and Body Language

Act is the blossom of thought, so as you change the way you think and elevate your thought processes, how you act will follow. But the reverse is also true to a degree as we noted in chapter five. How you act can change the general direction of your thoughts. Do you believe this?

Think about the last time you spoke in public. Or performed a karaoke song. Or conducted a seminar or made a presentation with a lot on the line. Or just were asked to introduce yourself to strangers. Were you nervous? Chapman University's list shows public speaking as the number one fear so if you get nervous heading to the mike, you're not alone. And if public speaking's the number one fear, where does public singing show up? No wonder karaoke usually only happens in cocktail lounges.

As you walk up to the mike, in any setting, most of us feel the nerves. It's just natural. And that adrenaline/cortisol blast can be leveraged to give you a more energetic opening followed by a deep and confident calm. Hopefully. We've all sat through an awkward presentation where the speaker comes out of the gate wobbling and never quite finds their voice or their posture and that can distract mightily from their message.

And as my debate coach impressed upon me years ago, you only look ten percent as nervous as you feel. Small comfort but there's some truth to that. And by acting less nervous than we might feel, we get a boost of confidence from that as well. This is important.

Your posture, your facial expression, the way you walk; all tend to follow or inspire how you feel. Walk confidently up to the mike and you'll feel more confident. Breathing's just so key to this process. If you take the mike and you're feeling the "fight or flight" syndrome, your breath will be coming in shallow gasps as that adrenaline and cortisol kicks in and physiological changes occur. This is the enemy if it persists, but your friend if you manage it as most experienced speakers do.

Take a deep breath or two and then connect your breaths coming out of that while in the "wings". Keep it up, consciously breathing in and then naturally exhale. This will calm you down somewhat and distract you from the outsized fear accompanying this exercise for many of us. You're not in nearly as much danger as your perception may indicate. In fact, this is an opportunity, isn't it? To entertain, persuade and move people. Just make sure you're standing tall, shoulders back, head up and hands relaxed, with palms open to your audience, not fidgeting.

Or use a couple of rounds of Dr. Andrew Weil's suggested calming technique in his four-seven-eight breathing routine. Four seconds breathing in through your nose, hold for seven and then eight seconds of exhaling through your mouth with your lips pursed. I've done this and just counted out to nineteen or twenty which, for me, seemed logical yet the four-seven-eight is easier at least for me. I trust Dr. Weil.

Just consciously focusing on your breathing will distract you from your nervousness to a degree which helps, and the breathing calms your thoughts considerably. But just continue to breathe in and out after a couple of these, connect those breaths in an orderly non-panicked manner.

And say this to yourself with sincerity in the hours leading up to the performance:

I am a genius, applying my wisdom to my public speaking skills.

Dan, you are a genius applying your wisdom to your public speaking skills.

Dan Wedin is a genius applying his wisdom to his public speaking skills.

I am a genius applying my wisdom to my powers of persuasion.

Dan, you are a genius applying your wisdom to your powers of persuasion.

Dan Wedin is a genius applying his wisdom to his powers of persuasion.

I am a genius applying my wisdom to my sense of humor.

Dan, you are a genius applying your wisdom to your sense of humor.

Dan Wedin is a genius applying his wisdom to his sense of humor.

Why do these work? I can only speak for myself but they do for me. My opinion is that when you are thinking right, you're acting right and you're performing better. It's the same mechanics used by counselors, coaches, teachers, mentors and those whose inner conversation is healthy, supportive and respectful. And most are experienced so it's an automatic reaction. They've built a well-myelinated neural pathway for this skill, after all. But if you're not used to doing this every day, one does not want to approach it in a half-hearted manner. If you're not going to try this honestly, I would suggest your results will not only vary, they'll quite likely be disappointing.

When your words are carefully chosen and you've practiced them until you're very comfortable with them you'll have gone a long way to silence the doubt and fear and insecurity. You're going to be more centered, more confident and much more likely to enjoy yourself. And who doesn't want to enjoy themselves? And that might be one of the great benefits of repeating these lines with some personal modifications that fit your needs. You end up exercising more control over your mood as you're limiting those drifts into negative thinking that can just dampen your enthusiasm for the task at hand. Who needs that?

So employ "posture consciousness" as you practice your mental conditioning. Soon it will be your habit to be sitting up straight, walking with excellent posture and feeling better as a result. Try this:

I am a genius applying my wisdom to walking with excellent posture.

Dan, you're a genius applying your wisdom to walking with excellent posture.

Dan Wedin's a genius applying his wisdom to walking with excellent posture.

I am a genius, applying my wisdom to every thought I think and action I take.

Dan, you are a genius applying your wisdom to every thought you think and action you take.

Dan Wedin is a genius applying his wisdom to every thought he thinks and every action he takes.

So yes, act is the blossom of thought, and thought can also be the blossom of action. Both intentional moves on your part can bear fruit. Facing a pressure situation? Gird yourself with a couple of minutes of powerful thinking, the "Superman Pose" (arms akimbo, shoulders back, chin up), the "Pride Pose" (arms up and hands reaching for the sky like you're crossing the finish line first), and your favorite breathing technique. Quality breathing helps you maintain the confidence and calm state of mind you're looking for here. And repeat your affs with feeling in these poses.

It can be helpful to watch others who carry themselves with authority, with a relaxed attitude, and with a bit of joy in their step. This is often the result of practice, training and experience rather than a natural skill. It's a learned skill, and anyone can learn it by building a positive, supportive and inspired neural pathway using strategic affs.

Yet you'll find yourself naturally mirroring this posture when you're breathing right, thinking right, and conscious of the body language you're transmitting. And the beautiful thing? Once you consciously begin work in this area it, too, becomes habitual as the myelin performs its magic. But remember the importance of feeling that sense of urgency and focus. That's the key to igniting the synapses that inspires the myelination and thus the growing skill.

Watch military personnel as they appear on television or online and you'll see the result of conscious efforts to project confidence, strength and composure. And movies and television shows demonstrate the power of "acting". In that case we're often watching an individual take it to another level and inhabit a completely different character.

When a skilled performer is "in character" it can be amazing to watch how it affects their body language, tone of voice and demeanor. I'm not suggesting you act, per se, but there will be times when it's necessary so fill the role. All the world's a stage, the Bard noted, and we are but actors upon it. As is often written, dress not for the job you've got, dress for the job you want. I think we can logically extend that philosophy to act not for where you find yourself in life, act for the life you really want and deserve.

Once you become familiar with your personal body language it will become very easy for you to detect posture that inspires or reflects weak or ineffective thinking. Slouch for a bit and feel the incongruity it presents to thinking with purpose and imagination. Stand, sit and walk straight and tall and see alternately how this affects your thought patterns and the feelings those thoughts engender.

You are the master of your soul, yes, but also your brain and your body. Once conscious of the impact these have on your life you're very likely to begin developing habits that make this, too, an area for self-improvement. You've nothing at all to lose and knowledge, power and confidence to gain.

For an in-depth look at body language and the importance of this essential part of your life, visit:

https://www.scienceofpeople.com/body-language/.

And wherever you are in life, give yourself the gift of confidence so to you it's just another appearance, not your first speech on the floor of the Senate, a legendarily intimidating venue that's shook solid public performers to their core. Few emerge having hit a home run the first time out, even those who go on to fame and acclaim.

You are the sum of your thoughts, so consider taking charge by practicing affs that support the outcome you desire. And if when saying those affs you allow a feeling of disbelief to take hold, stop and start over again. Address whatever's inhibiting you from moving forward with verve and a bit of panache. You've a role to play in this world, you have every right to be here and imagine the champagne effect of turning in a great performance that meets or exceeds your expectations and that of your audience.

Go ahead, your future beckons and awaits your coming. But you must meet it halfway. Stride confidently, happily in that direction. And then, as you grow, take the time to celebrate each victory and the wave of dopamine and other brain chemistry that brings you nothing but pure pleasure. In short bursts, of course. You deserve it, because yes, you've *earned* it. And it will motivate you onward to further victories and achievements.

In closing, remember what Marshall McLuhan taught us many years ago and that's that *"the medium is the message"*. You are the medium, how you carry yourself delivers a very clear message for better or worse. By cultivating your self-awareness you're halfway to exercising some wholesome control over this medium that is you.

So deliver the message you choose, not the one your subconscious defaults to. You are the medium and you are the message. Make it a powerful and confident one and don't just save it for the big things, practice it in your life, every day and in every way. You get one chance at a *"first impression"*, right? So be consistent and make that impression one that earns you notice and respect.

After all, you get one shot at this experience of life. It's yours and yours alone. Make the utmost of it every day in every way. You're going to change, anyway, so taking the wheel and directing that inevitable process can be highly enjoyable and satisfying. You'll note, at times, your progress, and the gratification you feel as you gain power and confidence will be exciting and inspire the kind of brain chemistry that will keep that very important growth on course. If you struggle here, try this:

I am a genius applying my wisdom to enjoying great faith in myself.

Dan, you are a genius applying your wisdom to enjoying great faith in yourself.

Dan Wedin is a genius applying his wisdom to enjoying great faith in himself.

Every day in every way I am feeling more faith in myself.

Every day in every way, Dan, you are feeling more faith in yourself.

Every day in every way Dan Wedin is feeling more faith in himself.

Say these with all of the zest and vigor and emotion and imagination you can muster. That skill, too, will grow, as your faith in yourself reaches full maturation. The faith others have in you is tied to the faith you have in yourself, after all. I have great faith that if you employ these affs faithfully yours will grow immeasurably and that will make your life eminently more enjoyable.

Again, why not?

Chapter Eight
Cultivating a Grateful Spirit

And the Happy Brain Chemistry it Inspires

"If you look at what you have in life, you'll always have more. If you look at what you don't have in life, you'll never have enough."

Oprah Winfrey

Once I was working on a writing project in the nineties and a thought occurred to me. I know the one thing that everybody wants! No matter their nationality, race, gender, religion and that one thing? More. More of something. Money, sex, security, success, happiness, enlightenment, sprituality, strength, peace, thrills, knowledge, power, recognition; everyone's in the market for more of something. And in the end it's simply a desire for more *Time*.

And this desire for more can be a force or it can be a gnawing clawing at the fabric of our lives giving us no rest. And no rest results in a weary soul yearning for peace of mind. Yet the wanting of more is inherently part of our nature, our mammalian nature, but inevitably tied to our need to survive and be secure. We're not going to turn that off under any circumstances. So where does that leave us?

Since the desire for more is an omni-present force, and it can be powerful and positive, let's temper it with a growing sense of gratefulness. When I was struck with cardiac arrest and forced to lay in the hospital for a week contemplating my predicament I was filled with a sense of gratefulness. *I was alive!* The description of what I'd been through coupled with my incomplete memory filled me with wonder. So there it was, I'd died and been revived. And I had a lot of my fellow human beings to thank for that.

Viewing it later as a *"movie in my mind"* I was no doubt inspired by my family and friends who compassionately visited and perhaps elevated in its intensity by the morphine drip alongside my hospital bed. That stuff was good. It reminded me of Dr. Watson's disapproval of Sherlock Holmes use of it between cases. I had empathy at this point for both points of view. And I had no idea of its role in my demeanor having gone unconscious and when I woke up I was under the influence. It seemed to be my new state of mind and I embraced it.

Yet by the time my lovely wife got me home a week later the effects began to wear off and all gratefulness evaporated. Now I had to take stock of my situation. Ah! Vicodin! Yes, once I was able to get ahead of the pain from my cracked sternum and fractured ribs sustained during CPR (*if you're not cracking ribs you're not doing it hard enough, one nurse told me*) I was again grateful for being alive. This was not lost on me. I liked the feeling of gratefulness for just being alive. I got a few laughs telling people I'd died and returned to heaven, as I've mentioned. A lot of truth in that.

So when I was fairly well healed and off the Vicodin I explored gratefulness and read a few essays. This heightened interest in gratefulness had me observing the people around me and I imagined I could tell who was grateful just by their demeanor. And I had a newfound appreciation for my wife as she really impressed me with the sense that hers were not occasional grateful feelings but a graceful style of simply being. I decided that was a very advanced state and one that I would benefit from emulating.

I thought of all the things for which I was grateful. It was quite a list and in its entirety I felt an even greater sense of well being and thankfulness. I'd been blessed and had certainly paid lip service to that but now I wanted to ascend to a higher plane of the feeling. Without the aid of drugs. Or did I?

In his book, *"Suggestible You"*, brilliant science writer, Erik Vance, titled his second chapter, *"Meet Your Inner Pharmacist"*. He opens the first page under the heading with a quote from the late and revered, Dr. Albert Schweitzer:

"Each patient carries his own doctor inside of him."

Vance proceeds to explore the brain and the chemistry at work in all of us. He explains that the brain has specific receptors adapted to receive and process opioids which he says partly explains their highly addictive nature to humans. And then he poses the question researchers faced: "Why would we have receptors for a drug that only exists in poppy plants? Unless...our brains make something like it as well."

Aha! So wait a second. If feeling grateful made me feel good, made my brain feel bathed in a joyous sensation, I was experiencing the self-dosing of opium from my brain's pharmacy. Once I was off the Vicodin, that is. And since we're regenerative organisms then there wasn't a limited amount on the shelf but rather an unending supply. I liked that thought. A lot.

But before you get a shot of dopamine in anticipation of learning how to unleash it permanently, it's available in short spurts only before reabsorption kicks in. So let's see if I can give you just a small sample of what I felt:

I am a genius applying my wisdom to my personal gratitude.

Dan, you are a genius applying your wisdom to your personal gratitude.

Dan Wedin is a genius applying his wisdom to his personal gratitude.

Every day in every way I grow more grateful.

Every day in every way, Dan, you grow more grateful.

Every day in every way Dan Wedin grows more grateful.

Dan Wedin is a genius applying his wisdom to being thankful for his life.

Dan Wedin is a genius applying his wisdom to living a life of gratefulness.

Keep this up and soon you may find yourself being grateful for feeling gratitude. I certainly do. This process and understanding of it can give rich new meaning to the term, *"High on Life"*. And there's a growing body of evidence that gratefulness woven into a work group can substantially increase job satisfaction and attendance while it tamps down antisocial behavior. And the mental changes it inspires can have a long lasting positive effect on the brain.

And yet we've all been "high on life" at times throughout our existence, haven't we? Think of all of the joyous and glorious times in your life when honestly? You never felt better. These periods are different for different people, of course, but the brain chemistry is the same.

Among the stocking items in your inner pharmacy are endocannabinoids, and yes, you read that root word right. They're the same class of chemicals marijuana contains. And serotonin, a driver of that inimitable feeling of well-being we strive for. Happiness is bathed in serotonin so anything we can do to prod our brain to release it is a good thing, isn't it? Gratitude definitely increases this important neurotransmitter and neuroscientists invoke *"Hebb's Law,"* which says that *"neurons that fire together, wire together,"* so adopting grateful habits consistently over time will blaze neural pathways that literally change your brain. For the better.

We're all aware of how easy it is to see in ourselves or others the habit of always seeing the bad in things, and we're all familiar with how difficult it is to change a bad habit. Yet by using *"You Are A Genius"* to foster an *"attitude of gratitude"* we can change that dynamic, lessening the negative hold of the bad habit, and inspiring neural connections that allow one to feel more mellow, more happy, and more at peace. You see, each change we make in the way we think alters the way the brain works on a subconscious level and added together produces a powerful and beneficial synergy. For life.

So I say most emphatically that yes, it is a good thing to not only take control of your feelings but to understand the nature of your inner pharmacy and become the chief pharmacist of your brain. Notably, depression is often characterized by a lack of serotonin which an entire class of pharmaceuticals attempts to spur into action. We can augment any treatment for depression, or ward it off, by increasing our serotonin levels and thus our well-being. Solitude can be a comfort but for the depressed it can be a further diminishing of the serotonin which will alleviate the condition. Stay in touch, be your own best friend and live a balanced life that includes the joys of an active social life.

Another neurochemical on the list is dopamine, as I've noted, and most of us are familiar with its profound effects. When endorphins are released during exercise or other events it increases the release of dopamine delivering at least some of the joy from that legendary *"runner's high"*. The one so good that I've read some runners with painful shin splints will run right through the pain to get to that pleasurable chemical release beyond dopamine to endorphin. That's not a good practice as endorphins are really there to make one oblivious to pain so inviting pain as a means to an end amounts to a slightly masochistic habit.

So I'm not going to get into a deeper treatment of brain chemistry, that's for others much more qualified. My goal is to simply help us acknowledge the fact that our feelings come from thoughts and actions which trigger the release of neurochemistry capable of improving our mood dramatically. Call it the "zone", "nirvana", "warm and fuzzies", "feeling good from head to toe", "ecstasy", "pure pleasure" or whatever aptly describes it for you. And to understand that the more we learn to habitually control our thoughts, the better the chemistry and so the better one's life.

"We are not thinking machines that feel, but feeling machines that think."

Dr. Antonio Damasio, Neuroscientist

And a big part of encouraging these good-feeling chemicals is avoiding the ones that make us feel bad, such as cortisol. Cortisol in surges is the fear feeling, the fight or flight syndrome with the adrenaline rush; when it simply drips it's anxiety or a slight panic. Cortisol is released in anticipation of pain, so learning to understand the difference between real pain and some perceived threat that on reflection is no threat at all to your survival, allows you to begin the process of avoiding undue stress.

If act is the blossom of thought then it follows that feeling is the fruit of that blossom. *Thought + Action = Feeling.* And intuitively we all know this is true. We know that when we hug someone we have feelings for we get a pleasurable rush, that's why we do it again and again. We repeat behaviors, if we're so inclined and most of us are, that make us happy and help us release the neurotransmitters dopamine, oxytocin, serotonin and endorphins.

"When I do good I feel good, when I do bad I feel bad, and that's my religion."

Abraham Lincoln, quoted in "Herndon's Lincoln", though Herndon stated that Lincoln attributed the quote to a "Glenn in Indiana". Thanks, Glenn.

Pretty simple when stated thusly, isn't it? Do good and you dispense chemicals that unerringly elevate your spirit making you feel good. And, of course, vice versa. If I've said this once, I've said it a million times, *"There is no joy in life like serving others."* My offspring's eyeballs will roll skyward should they read this book; they've heard it all before.

A friend once noted over lunch that I seemed to have a neurotic desire to seek approval through my copywriting. I didn't disagree though I wouldn't have put it quite like that. When a client needed the right words at the right time to achieve an objective and I produced them? Yeah, I got a charge, think positive brain chemistry, out of that. At a certain point I realized it was as important to me as the money paid to me for the service.

Keep in mind that this is fairly common knowledge and don't think marketers anxious to get you to stay on their site, linger in a store, buy things and rate experiences don't know this. So understand that yes, you can exercise some control over this chemical matrix but so can others. So when you're made to feel pleasure while visiting a site, store or restaurant, playing one of their little games, getting a reward, feeling more pleasure; there may be an ulterior motive. As a student of Sir Arthur Conan Doyle and his brilliant Sherlock Holmes, I'm always on the lookout for ulterior motives. They surround us even as we exercise our own.

So yes, thinking good thoughts is a good habit to cultivate and thinking good thoughts about how grateful you are for everything is an excellent one. When you're bathed in gratefulness your heart is full, your brain is releasing pleasurable chemistry and you're encouraged to continue in this vein.

You may want to consider making affs of gratefulness and the resulting feelings a daily habit, one you can grow and feel flourish. The deeper you go, the more it becomes a way of life and a grateful life is a great one. But remember, it may take time to really sink the habit into your subconscious so stay with it via intense focus and celebrate even the smallest of victories, or feelings, along the way.

Every day in every way my heart is filled with grateful feelings.

Every day in every way, Dan, your heart is filled with grateful feelings.

Every day in every way Dan Wedin's heart is filled with grateful feelings.

I suggest you consider making feeling grateful your life's work. Oh, you'll have time for plenty of other things, and they will provide you with ever more reasons for gratitude if you're advancing in your life's work, won't they? Amor fati, love it all. Every bit of it. And if at first you struggle, understand that this is okay and to be expected. Begin with simple, straightforward acceptance.

"Wear gratitude like a cloak and it will feed every corner of your life."

Rumi, Persian Scholar and Poet, 13th Century

Just know that when you learn to love the seemingly unloveable elements of your life because they are part of your life? You will free yourself of much strife and inner ill will and a sense of release and relief will come over you as you revel in being grateful for everything. Everything. Amor fati, after all.

Now one might postulate that okay, it's easy for you, Dan, to feel grateful. You said yourself you *"died and returned to heaven!"* That's true, but does that mean that one has to face a near death experience to tap into the awesome power and wonderful feelings of living a grateful life? No, and of course you knew that would be my reaction. After all, we can't set up near death experiences for everyone to trigger this experience, can we? Hmm. Let's try a simple exercise.

And remember? It's not where you are, it's the state you're in. So how do we change one's current state from taking life for granted to feeling a semi-searing sense of gratefulness for being alive? One that occasionally makes you want to just kick up your heels and grin or let out a yay-YAY-*YAY!* Let's start a list, even if it's just a mental one. Think of all of the memories of your life. But focus on one. Which one?

Has anyone close to you ever died? I would imagine that would be answered in the affirmative for the vast majority of us. Okay, write down the names. For some the list may be surprisingly long. The older you grow the more this seems to happen, doesn't it? We take these events individually and mourn our loss but in this instance let's treat this as a group.

My Grandfather

My Best Friend

My Mother

My Father

My Grandmother

A Brother-in-Law

A Brother-in-Law

My Wife's Mother

My Best Friend

A Brother-n-Law

My Wife's Father

Me (tbd)

Okay, once you have your list complete or fairly complete, stop. Now add yourself. Use your full name and add the "(tbd)" or "to be determined". In my case I have a sense that just about everyone's going to outlive me, after all, a cardiologist did use the very precise time frame (in terms of mortality) of "five years". Yet none of us really knows from one day to the next when the grand finale occurs. And for most of us it is not a grand departure at all. It can be sad, painful, tragic, unthinkable, devastating; state it in your own language.

It can happen slowly as we circle the drain in an ill despair. It can happen over time as the result of natural forces. It can happen in an instant when you're traveling in any kind of conveyance whatsoever, even on an innocent bicycle. Life happens and so does death. I read the paper, I see things, I hear things. It's just the reality of human existence.

It's coming. And if you look at the insurance industry's actuarial tables it's not hard to count it in months in the absence of other threatening factors. People are going to do what people are going to do and one of the things they do is die. Just a fact of life, the most certain one of all.

"This is our big mistake: to think we look forward to death. Most of death is already gone. Whatever time has passed is owned by death."

Seneca 4 BC – 65 AD

Embrace your mortality. Know that generations come and go. Know that this is a law no one, not the wisest, wealthiest or most cunning among us can escape. It is an immutable fact. If your ambition is to live forever it's a fool's errand. But if your ambition is to live your life with good health, grateful for life and in service to your fellow humans? Embark on that noble journey today if you're not already underway.

"Do as much as you can, as well as you can, for as many as you can, for as long as you can."

John Wesley, Founder of the Methodist Church 1703-1791

Ideally one would enjoy as high a degree of health as their habits, genes and fate would allow them and then to live to a ripe old age and die in their sleep after a happy day of laughter and love.

That's perhaps a pipe dream, isn't it? An uncommon exit but if you stop and think about it there are a number of factors within our control that will allow us to make that noble attempt. I heartily endorse that goal and cheer you on to success. That is a wonderful ideal. Why not?

But there's one thing about that wonderful ideal, isn't there? It still ends in your demise. And this must be faced and embraced. This is part of your fate as a human being on this planet. And perhaps the strongest reason to explore that *"Amor Fati"*, or a love of one's fate. This "Stoic" philosophy has been espoused by the towering German philosopher Friedrich Nietzsche and in earlier times by the Stoics Roman Emperor Marcus Aurelius and the born-into-slavery and physically afflicted philosopher Epictetus. As well as the vastly wise Seneca, the Roman philosopher, statesman and writer.

This love of one's fate frees you from the regrets, resentments and pain of the past, the dissatisfaction with the present and dread of the future. In modern vernacular one might take the simple modern phrase, *"It's all good"* and see in it the tenets of Stoic philosophy.

Stoicism doesn't supplant one's religion or other philosophical beliefs, it simply informs them with an attitude that allows for gratefulness for all things in one's life. The good, the bad, the ugly. The painful, the losses, the failures. They are part of one's unique life, one's unique and growing perspective and they are what gives each of us a distinctly valuable voice in the general human discourse.

George Satayana, the Spanish philosopher and writer taught us:

"There is no cure for birth and death save to enjoy the interval."

So love the fact that you were born! You belong here, it is your loveable fate. And love the fact that you will die, and behold and love your posterity, it is all you'll truly leave behind. And it will be forgotten at some point just as the powerful poetry of an earlier age and a defunct language is lost in the dust of time past.

So ponder this moment, and love your present regardless of your current circumstances and embrace the fact that sooner or later you will join that dust and its overwhelming anonymity. Leaving you with what?

Nothingness, save whatever hopes you may entertain of an "afterlife". Love those thoughts and feelings, too, but let them not distract you from your rapture with the present.

Santayana understood amor fati, and expounded on it brilliantly:

"Happiness is the only sanction of life; where happiness fails, existence remains a mad and lamentable experiment."

I cannot speak for you, dear human being, but I can tell you I want no part of being a *"mad and lamentable experiment"*. Though critics of this book may indeed turn that noble quote against me. I promise to love it when the brickbats fly!

So accept yourself, accept your life, accept your thoughts. And slowly, inexorably advance to love all of it, every single iota of your existence. You'll grow in gratefulness and be thankful to yourself that you embarked on this, the greatest and most beneficial adventure and journey of your life. The feelings you'll feel! The rushes you'll experience! And the peace of mind you'll enjoy. We might want to call an element of this achieving *"greatfulness"*. Hey, why not?

So I must deal with a nagging thought. Am I presenting this as if I've completed and mastered this journey, this epic of human emotion and feeling? No, quite the contrary. It's just that the journey, one which many, many of my fellow humans are far ahead of me on, opens up doors to wonder, hallways of light and promise, and daily new dawns of opportunity in which to grow, flourish and relish the wonderful construct that is the human brain. Tap it for all its worth!

There are many paths on which to find your Joie de Vivre. But let's face it, few will make you as happy as quickly and as lastingly as nurturing the feeling that is within all of us. Don't fall into the trap of *"lip service"*, of telling others how grateful you *"truly"* are. Sometimes I feel the more I hear someone tell me how grateful they are the less it seems so. Live it, practice it, display it and absolutely leverage its power to flood your brain with the chemistry that will give you the feelings you deserve. The ones in which you want to be immersed for the rest of your days. But understand that it's a journey, so strive to experience gratitude ever more deeply and with ever more emotion and conviction every day in every way.

I am a genius applying my wisdom to my growing gratefulness.

Dan, you are a genius applying your wisdom to your growing gratefulness.

Dan Wedin is a genius applying his wisdom to his growing gratefulness.

Or perhaps you might find a slightly different version more effective at engendering a feeling. This entire exercise is a voyage of discovery so whenever you discover something that works for you, take a deep dive into the thoughts and affs that drive that feeling.

I am a genius, applying my wisdom to growing my gratefulness.

Dan, you are a genius applying your wisdom to growing your gratefulness.

Dan Wedin is a genius applying his wisdom to growing his gratefulness.

It is not the man who has too little, but the man who craves more, that is poor.

If a man knows not to which port he sails, no wind is favorable.

Seneca

Let's take Seneca's wisdom and make it our own and set sail for the sunny shore of Gratefulness. It's waiting for us, and it's a reachable destiny. And the journey there promises to be the Trip of a Liftetime...

You Are A GENIUS

You Are A GENIUS

It's not where you are, it's the state you're in.

Chapter Nine
Your Personal Power

Nothing is more powerful than an idea whose time has come.

Victor Hugo, French Writer 1885-1941

Okay, I found this quote in more than one form. Perhaps *"Nothing's stronger than an idea whose time has come"*, has a better claim to accuracy, but the one above strikes a more resonant tone to my ear.

I might steal Mr. Hugo's line here and state that it's also true that nothing's more powerful than a self-empowered person whose time has come. The dream lies before them, the challenges are at present unmet. Yet the individual who's decided that this is their time, this is their place and then uses each moment and empowered thinking to advance their cause? *Unstoppable.*

Events in life at times leave us feeling powerless, or nearly powerless. There is a finite nature, after all, to what we can control. As I've noted, people are going to do what people are going to do. But we know we can exercise some wholesome discretion over how we react. And importantly, whether we react at all, because sometimes your reaction is the only thing keeping someone acting out in a particular way.

And feelings of powerlessness, hopelessness and helplessness are the enemy in life. They leave you distraught and depressed. A wise person once said that depression is rage spread thin and that struck a chord with me. But perhaps the worst element of powerlessness is that it has a profound effect on one's immune response and that's backed up by science.

In his fascinating book which I've previously mentioned, an international best seller, *"Anticancer, A New Way of Life"*, Dr. David Servan-Schreiber, a brain cancer victim, found himself searching for answers, for clues, for inspiration when his cancer returned six years later. His research led him to explore an array of cases, of treatments and some intriguing advanced methodology and thought.

No one who gets cancer is to blame for this, he emphatically declares. He notes that:

"It usually takes from five to forty years for the bad "seed" of cancer in the form of a cellular anomaly, to become a detectable cancerous tumor. During this process, cells that were initially healthy become seriously malfunctional, due to abnormal genes, or, much more commonly, exposure to radiation, environmental toxins or other toxins such as benzopyrene from cigarette smoke."

He continues:

"I must insist on one point: No psychological factor by itself has ever been identified as being capable of creating that bad seed. In other words, nothing permits us to state that psychic trauma can be the sole cause of cancer."

Yet there is evidence that environmental factors can profoundly influence the physical conditions in which the seed finds itself. And one of those factors is the patient's mental state and whether they're in the throes of recovering from a traumatic event. I don't want to get into this issue too deeply here but his book is one that's well worth your time. Filled with cutting edge information as one would expect from a physician with a PhD who is dedicated to research. And one who's faced a deadly brain tumor and beat it. Twice.

Though we're all aware of the impact of our attitude on our health, aren't we? Most of us have experienced catching a cold prior to a major event and just powering through with grit and will until the mission's accomplished at which point the full force of the rhinovirus takes hold. But the mission has been accomplished.

And perhaps you've also experienced that cold that can lay you low when you're not in the best of moods and you just succumb to the effects. I've found myself fighting a cold and throwing vitamin C, chicken bone broth with hot sauce, extra garlic pills, Ashwagandha and more at it. And I've found in multiple instances that the cold I've caught's minimal and gone in two or three days where those around me battle it for a week or more. Allied with the external factors I'm applying is a conscious thought, *"I'm not letting this virus beat me!"* After all, my late Father did call me *"Bucky Beaver Pirate Fighter"*. Thanks, Dad.

My point is that it's very well documented that those who give up find whatever they're battling takes its cue from a weakened system and strengthens. And those who fight it tend to enjoy more success in the course of events. And this goes way beyond physical health issues. Regardless, there are many, many other beneficial reasons to develop a strong sense of personal power. Life can be difficult at times and absolutely brutal at other junctures. Let's use the power of *"You Are A Genius"* to leverage existing knowledge to grow stronger.

Act is the blossom of thought and one way to develop your personal power is to think empowering thoughts and to carry yourself with a sense of personal power. We've all seen the weak shrink into a room, apologetically, and looking as helpless and hapless as they feel.

Were that person to walk in confidently, even if they didn't feel completely confident, we'd have quite the different impression, wouldn't we? Remember Mr. Gibbs' admonition in debate: *You only look ten percent as nervous as you feel.* Plus your brain will definitely follow your body if you decide to breathe, walk, talk and carry yourself with confidence.

Yes, act is the blossom of thought, yet thought can also, at times, be the blossom of your actions. Act strong in the face of a crisis and your brain will cooperate. Act broken and powerless in that circumstance and your brain responds accordingly, sinking you further into the depths of despair. Yet this, too, can be beneficial, can't it? Those who truly break down and descend to the depths of mourning when the crisis is the tragic loss of a loved one eventually hit bottom at some point and then what happens? They rise again, having healthily felt the pain, experienced the grief, and wallowed in self-pity. As usual, it's complicated. So we persist.

Cheesily, an old motivational speaker used to say *"fake it until you make it."* Maybe I'm being harsh in calling it cheesy but that's how it struck me the first time I read it. But I do think there is some truth to this and I've seen it in practice. I've had friends and associates who've confessed to me great trepidation prior to a speech or presentation and yet when I watch them perform I have trouble detecting that.

And there's a momentum factor at work here, once you get going and you realize no one's laughing or jeering and a flaming arrow or rotten tomato hasn't hit you, it gets noticeably easier to confidently perform.

I saw a TED Talk once that I found intriguing. Actually, many, but this one's pertinent. This presenter talked about how she overcame so much physically and mentally after a horrific automobile accident to achieve her success. One of her techniques was to mimic the *"International Victory Symbol"*, also known as *"Pride"* or the *"Pride Pose"* prior to challenging presentations. The technique this woman, Professor Amy Cuddy, suggests is simply to stand with your arms extended triumphantly upward in a "V" with your chin lifted for a couple of minutes. She suggests doing it in private in a restroom. Try that prior to your next challenge. And google, *"TED Talk Amy Cuddy"* and consider viewing it now. It's worth every second of your time, trust me, as I've already noted. She relates a poignant and valuable story in a most engaging fashion.

And try this while maintaining that pose:

I am a genius applying my wisdom to my belief in my personal power.

Dan, you are a genius applying your wisdom to your belief in your personal power.

Dan Wedin

Dan Wedin is a genius applying his wisdom to his belief in his personal power.

I am a genius applying my wisdom to my Personal Power.

Dan, you are a genius applying your wisdom to your Personal Power.

Dan Wedin is a genius applying his wisdom to his Personal Power.

Every day in every way my Personal Power grows.

Every day in every way, Dan, your Personal Power grows.

Every day in every way Dan Wedin's Personal Power grows.

Dan Wedin is a genius applying his wisdom to experiencing personal power.

Your sense of personal power is a complex blend of recurring thoughts and habits that either work for or against you. Often we're plagued by thought loops or deep feelings with no description attached that we're oblivious to that drag us down, hold us back and sometimes sell who and what we are short. It's an element, a primal one, in the battle to be one's own best friend. And if you're going to aspire to genius thoughts, actions and initiatives on the way to achieving your goals and dreams, having yourself as an ally's a must, isn't it?

Your best friend wouldn't say some of the things we often think. Isn't that curious? We wouldn't think of them as best friends if they spoke to us like that yet we put up with it from ourselves. This is something we can change, something we want to change and definitely a behavioral trait we want to leave in our wake. I'm not talking about rooting those thoughts out, I'm suggesting we replace them with better thinking. And better feelings. *Auto-suggestion can help you weaken their hold on your mind by supplanting them with better thinking.*

If you imagine your brain as a series of boxes with each containing a specific portion of your life, imagine there's a neural pathway to each box. Which paths are the most well-worn in your brain? Now imagine you put a brand new box up there and it's empty. You begin a new thought process based on some of the techniques in this book. And visualize this box as special, as adorned in a way you find attractive and memorable. And make the lid easy to lift and access at all times.

The more you exercise the neural pathway to these aggregated thoughts, the more myelin it will exhibit, and the stronger and more efficient that neural pathway becomes. And hence the less traffic is experienced and felt on the path to the box with the negative thoughts you don't want to think but seemingly cannot avoid. This happens as the pathway to those thoughts you've strategically chosen brightens and strengthens. And the path to the debilitating thoughts weakens and fades. This is supplanting at its best.

In the metaphor of "brain boxes", they all have lids. One opens the box, examines and feels the contents and when done the lid is replaced and the next topic "box" is opened. Sounds logical but in reality let's face it, sometimes the box lid doesn't fit tightly, or comes blowing off. And in the full force of this lack of control over the boxes all of the lids come off and all of the contents come flying out. This, of course, is insanity.

So let's install a new box, a new file folder, a new niche. Use whatever analogous concept with which you're most comfortable. And visualize taking those boxes whose contents you'd like to view less frequently and pile a few rocks on the lid by devoting more and more time to strong thinking that honors your spirit and strengthens you and helps release the kind of brain chemistry that drives you to your own personal bliss. Myelinate those neural pathways leading to happiness and accomplishment!

The first thing we want to make sure of is that we have faith in our ability to change our thinking. How will we make our dreams come true, how will we achieve our goals if we're not becoming, through the process of change, that person capable of achieving these lofty goals and dreams? The short answer is we can't. We'll shrink from those victories if we feel unworthy of playing that role.

And yet, though we cling at times to the misguided thought that we cannot change, the reality is we're a living, breathing, aging human being and change is, in fact, the only constant. We have to change in some ways, we have to make adjustments, the people around us change, and so many other things change around us as we navigate our way through the seas of life.

Yes, you can change, you are changing, all one needs to do is take a wholesome control of that change dynamic as it's going to happen anyway. Wouldn't it be wise to direct that inevitable process of change to benefit you? Of course it would. It's already happening so make the decision to exercise a bit of personal control over this ongoing and inescapable process.

So let's embrace change, that constant that is in play whether we recognize or want to admit it or not. Think of every day as a new mini-life, one you can craft for your pleasure and benefit. It's a simple matter of deciding to be proactive instead of reactive:

I am a genius applying my wisdom to my Personal Power of Change.

Dan, you are a genius applying your wisdom to your Personal Power of Change.

Dan Wedin is a genius applying his wisdom to his Personal Power of Change.

Every day in every way I am changing for the better.

Every day in every way, Dan, you are changing for the better.

Every day in every way Dan Wedin is changing for the better.

Okay, I hear a little voice in the back of the room saying come on, Dan, I don't like the changes that come with getting older! I get that. But look at it this way. We have a life, sure, but we also have many, many chapters in the story of this life. You're writing part of the tale right now by choosing, for whatever reason, to read this book. And don't look at your entire life and compare yourself physically to an earlier gestation of yourself. That's self-defeating. Amor fati, right?

Age is an issue of mind over matter. If you don't mind, it doesn't matter.

Mark Twain

You've never been where you're at right at this moment so make the very most of it. Be the best version of you at your age that you can be. Make this chapter of your life the one with the most love and pleasure and growth. Why not?

When asked what age they'd select if they had to live their rest of their life at that point the vast majority select the age they are today. Forever 21 is declaring bankruptcy, literally and figuratively. If you're depressed with your age, contemplate yourself as fixed in time forever. That's where the dearly departed are, right? You're still in the game so make sure you're still playing it as high a level as you possibly can. And never stop looking for ways to grow and improve.

If you've children, grandchildren, loved ones or nieces and nephews think about how much you hope for the best for them! You want them safe, you want them to grow, you want them to find love and happiness. Don't you deserve the same thing? Of course you do but if you're not confident in that idea then this is a negative that you want to supplant with some powerful thoughts.

I am a genius applying my wisdom to supporting myself in ALL that I do.

Dan, you are a genius applying your wisdom to supporting yourself in ALL that YOU do.

Dan Wedin is a genius applying his wisdom to supporting himself in ALL that HE does.

Of course, if you're involved in self-destructive behavior you want to be aware of this and not support the furtherance of what's destroying your health or mental vitality. If you have doubts about this and aren't able to differentiate good from bad behavior seek help through counseling or just have a talk with your primary care physician about how you're feeling or habits you have that are difficult to change. They have access to the help you know you want and need.

So do seek help and there are resources in your life designed to help you, but you do have to ask. You can never get what you don't ask for, right? If you have needs that you can't meet, seek help. Miracles happen when we ask for help so do not hesitate. I suggest you consider doing it right now.

If you're addicted to something it is not because you're a bad person. It's simply brain chemistry at work. The drugs deliver the dopamine at such incredible levels that it becomes irresistible. It takes help in the vast majority of cases so seek that help. Do it now. The will to do comes from the knowledge that we can do and if you don't have that knowledge yet, believe it. And ask for the help you need.

And in conjunction with those efforts custom design an aff specifically for the behavior you want to change. Let's say your drinking habits are teetering out of control, something that's not uncommon over time. After all, one seeks a certain feeling with any mind altering substance and the drug alcohol is no different. And over time it can take more and more of this drug to achieve this effect.

I am a genius applying my wisdom to enjoying myself without alcohol.

Dan, you are a genius applying your wisdom to enjoying yourself without alcohol.

Dan Wedin is a genius applying his wisdom to enjoying himself without alcohol.

I am a genius applying my wisdom to drinking in moderation.

Dan, you are a genius applying your wisdom to drinking in moderation.

Dan Wedin is a genius applying his wisdom to drinking in moderation.

Feel free to write your own aff in your own words using the *"I am a genius applying my wisdom..."* opening. Then experiment until you find one that strikes that mental note, the one you can truly feel, for that's the one that will blaze a new neural pathway with the least effort. Once you've established the words just repeat them multiple times daily with as much focus and intensity as you can muster. And heighten their effectiveness by saying them on rising or soon after and before you nod off for the night. If it sounds like there are going to be too many things to remember to say, print out your lines, write them out, record them. Yet you may find that this is not necessary.

The reason I predict this will be less of an issue than you might imagine is simple human nature. After a few weeks of daily practice you'll find these become so habitual as to become involuntary making additional lines easy to add. And you'll be surprised how much time you currently spend thinking thoughts that are useless or nearly so. And this habit is also a powerful tool in the drive for mindfulness, trust me on that.

This is also a good time to take inventory of the quality of conversation going on inside your head. These can be very deeply rooted and difficult to thwart so just start with awareness and acknowledgment. And during this process, breathe. Yes, just breathe. Consciously breathe in and then just let your breath out naturally, connecting the next breath to that exhale. If you need help with this read this short description of *"Vivation"*. The word springs from the Latin, *"vive"*, or life. Here's the link spelled out:

http://vivation.com/inspiration/articles/the-five-elements-of-vivation/

Write down thoughts you'd rather not think, thoughts that do not honor or empower you. Rooting them out can be a chore, a thorny, intricate task at which you may or may not succeed. Or you may recognize them, temporarily slow them down and then on a bad day give in to our frenemy, habit.

Better to simply supplant those thoughts with good thoughts. You love yourself, right? Love thy neighbor as thyself, right? I struggled with this as when I was a boy *"self love"* was seen as *"selfish"* and the wrong way to view oneself. When I got out into the world that view widened and was informed by some prime examples of healthy *"self love"*. I thank them for that, it was a seminal period in my life. Okay, let's see if we can inspire some good brain chemistry here:

I am a genius applying my wisdom to loving myself.

Dan, you are a genius applying your wisdom to loving yourself.

Dan Wedin is a genius applying his wisdom to loving himself.

When I first began using this line with various endings I found it to be remarkably inspirational. As opposed to just letting one's thoughts drift to various random points dot com? Of course it would be, wouldn't it? Think of it as prayer without theology woven in. And the further you go, with emotion and urgency of course, the more you myelinate the neural pathways on which these lines travel. And that's a good thing as it means those accumulating wraps of myelin on that nerve path just make the thought fast, effective and perfectly timed.

Don't fight forces, use them, and craft your neural pathways as they are indeed the skills you own, and the skills you will be known for to yourself and others.

And for those who are plagued with the debilitating feeling that they need to be perfect, take a long, hard look at that. Really? To be loved you have to be perfect? Do you impose that judgment on the people you love? Woe to your relationships if that's the case.

Never let perfect be the enemy of good. If you're cleaning your homespace and you spend two hours it will look fine. Perfect? No, but fine. But if you spend five hours, wow, you can get it *"perfect"*. Will anyone but you notice? Most likely not and those three magically golden hours have slipped away from you. Again. Relax, do things well and then move on to some other productive or enjoyable activity. All you really have is time so guard it jealously. You want every minute to count, don't you? Even if it's just for some simple, soothing solitude.

That's not to say that there's nothing you want to do with the clearly stated goal of perfection in mind. But make that the absolute exception, not the rule. And relax a bit. Powerful people are relaxed, nonchalant and yet driven to self-improvement. The statement, "Don't sweat the small stuff," is very popular, but it misses something important in my mind. As a writer, editing one's work is all about paying attention to details, so make it clear in your own mind what constitutes the so-called, *"small stuff"*.

Love yourself wherever you are on your growth journey. Take good care of yourself. Pamper yourself when you need it. And always speak to yourself in loving, respectful tones. Now, there may be times when you need a good self-talking to, it's certainly been true in my case. But be forgiving, be thankful and be your own best friend. From morning to night. It's all about the love and that includes the love you feel for yourself.

You deserve this and it helps support your goal of strengthening your Personal Power. How? You deserve to have no doubt that you're on your own side, which solidifies your stance in life. After all, if you're not in good standing with yourself, how will the rest of the world react to you?

And while we may ridicule those who practice *"illeism"*, the act of referring to oneself in the third person, it's been scientifically proven to be beneficial psychologically, helping you to separate yourself a bit from yourself, informing your perspective with a different viewpoint. You'll note that one of the foundations of *"You Are A Genius"* is the *"I, You, She"*, *"I, You, He"* format to the affs. Try focusing on the third person a bit. How does that strike you? You may not want to use the third person in public, though, as some find it oddly offensive.

Speaking to yourself in the third person is a form of self-distancing and gives us a measure of control over our emotions and helps thwart that ominous spiral downward into thought patterns that instigate the release of chemistry that is just not the kind we want to encourage. Let the world trigger the release of those dreaded feelings, don't inspire them yourself. And limit their effect chronologically. Let them pass without following that inclination to take immediate action to counteract the panicky feeling. Tell yourself in the third person you don't succumb to that rut of helplessness.

As an exercise, try this, inserting your name, of course:

Dan Wedin is dedicated to gaining Personal Power.

Dan Wedin is a genius, applying his wisdom to his Personal Power.

What is Dan Wedin going to think to grow his Personal Power?

What will Dan Wedin do today to grow his Personal Power?

Dan Wedin enjoys the feeling his Personal Power gives him.

Dan Wedin knows an important part of Personal Power is humility.

How can Dan Wedin improve the world with his Personal Power?

In his book, *"Money Is My Friend"*, the late Phil Laut employs the first, second and third person in his highly detailed and wide-ranging affirmations. As I read the book I found some of them really tweaked something in my brain. When I received the book I was the marketing director of a twenty-five station radio group and gave frequent presentations to ad agencies and direct clients. And of course not every presentation or meeting or lunch resulted in an agreement. His advice, and I referred to this earlier:

"I now understand that 'No' means I decline your offer, I love you, I admire you, I respect you, and I am open to future offers."

Hee! Yes, I have mentioned this prior, but when I first read this line it made me laugh out loud, as I also noted in a previous chapter. It was such an unorthodox point of view to me, but I liked it. It's not what happens, it's your reaction. It's not where you are, it's the state you're in. That line truly eliminated the fear of rejection while trying to sell all of the network's available airtime. And I wasn't really struggling with the feeling, as I operated under the m.o. of *"You can't get what you don't ask for,"* which assumes rejection but encourages you to just play the numbers game.

But this sense that it wasn't a matter of personal rejection at all, it was a matter of timing, was quite empowering. Another example of it's not what happens it's one's reaction that truly counts. It isn't all about us, it's often what's happening to the person we're dealing with that we cannot know. No one can truly know the machinations, the trials and tribulations another faces. But we can be empathetic and simply move on. Time is precious so focus your time on where you can have the most impact.

So are you feeling more powerful after reading this chapter? If you'd like to delve deeper into this topic, Michael Korda's interesting book, *"Power, How To Get It, How To Use It"* might prove of value. And if you Google that and end up at the library, in a bookstore or on Amazon you'll find a plethora of other titles dealing with the analysis, strategies, and implications of power at all levels.

But do commit yourself to coming to grips with your personal power or lack thereof. And then commit yourself to allowing yourself to feel your personal power, grow your personal power and revel in the small but important victories that will be yours once you explore, practice and develop this most important human quality. An empowered group of human beings is an indomitable force and the challenges we face as a species demand we exercise our powers to overcome what are, without question, daunting tasks.

To your Personal Power! Seize it! You deserve it. And just think of all the good a stronger, more powerful and assertive You could do. You might not change the whole world but by changing your world for the better you can have impact, and a happier life and thus this will, in fact, make the world a better place. And that is my wish for you. Why not you? *And why not now?*

You Are A GENIUS

It's not where you are, it's the state you're in.

Chapter Ten
Back To Your Future

If you've read this deep into this slim volume it's possible that you've examined your goals, your objectives, and the dream that you'll realize once you achieve those. If so, why not begin the process of weaving those into your daily thought patterns and beginning the great adventure that awaits you when you do actually bring that dream to vivid fruition?

So where do you start? You already have, actually. As you repeat Coue's line daily you're preparing your brain and its thought processes, and you're getting better and better every day. This positions you for success for all of your goals big and small. When every thought you think changes you and you consistently return to thinking empowering, uplifting thoughts, you grow as a human being. That's the growth necessary for you to match up with living that dream.

And that's important. It's like physical training in advance of a game or a season. Every lift, every mile, every specialized practice technique moves you forward even if it's not a replication of the actual game itself for which you're training. But it builds strength, endurance, mental discipline and the inimitable esteem that's drawn from the accomplishment of small goals enroute to the bigger prize.

Yet we can sharpen our focus as we actually play the game in question, can't we? In this case we want to incorporate the language of each objective on the path to achieving goals that when taken in total make the realization of your dream inevitable. For every dream of any size and merit involves many facets, many challenges, and often withering obstacles standing right in the damn way. We just want to make sure that we, ourselves, are not one of those obstacles.

And that last factor happens more than we might imagine. Yes, we hold the dream dear but can allow doubt, fear, negativity and a lack of perseverance to thwart our efforts to succeed. One might make a strong case for the fact that often the greatest satisfaction derived from making a dream come true is in overcoming internal rather than external factors.

But once you envision your dream, picture the goals and objectives required, you can preemptively disable any internal opposition from factors in your vast subconscious. So how does one do that? After all, the opposition internally might be hidden, obscure and largely unknowable.

Perhaps it's an obvious factor which makes it easy to address with auto-suggestion and strategically thought-out affs. But let's say it's not something you can put your finger on. It's very possible it exists on a subconscious level and is not expressed lingually which would reveal its nature. Remember that the cortex thinks in words, the limbic brain in emotion. And emotions can be vague feelings that we just know are true, right? Think gut feelings. Fine. Address that vitally important faith in yourself:

Every day in every way my faith in myself grows.

Dan, every day in every way your faith in yourself grows.

Every day in every way Dan Wedin's faith in himself grows.

Which of those struck a chord you could feel? For me, for whatever reason, the third person has the most impact, yet I choose to say all three and perhaps repeat the third more than once. This has led me to often say the third person version first and often only. But that's just me. Say these lines to yourself or out loud each morning and return to it during the day and then give it a strong finish prior to turning in.

Your brain during sleep has many functions that we now know can spur more activity than when you're awake watching television. And while natural physiological processes are at work, the subconscious is also answering questions and making neural connections, all while you dream of rowing across a lake full of jumping goldfish.

By inputting an empowering thought before retiring you're suggesting to your brain that there's something you'd like to improve, something you'd like to grow. Pursuant to my story about the Maui resort radio spot, I was once a busy freelance writer with cash flow issues. I had a solid accounts receivable list but clients who paid on their schedule regardless of the *"due upon receipt"* line on my invoice. One night before retiring I asked myself, *"How can I get out of this temporary cash flow fix?"*

I went to bed and as soon as I woke the thought of partially billing a client for whom I was in the middle of a major project occurred to me. When I arrived in my office I picked up the phone and called the client and asked if I could bill for half the project upfront. No problem, she told me, want to pick up a check today? Voila! So will it work that fast every time? I would guess not but it's worth the slight effort involved, wouldn't you agree?

So in the grand scheme of officially going after your dream, objective by objective, goal by goal, obstacle by obstacle, keep the "Big Question" technique in your back pocket, it may come in handy.

So develop an aff for your overriding objective, the dream you want to reach after accomplishing a series of smaller goals.

I am a genius applying my wisdom to building a great business.

Dan, you are a genius applying your wisdom to building a great business.

Dan Wedin is a genius applying his wisdom to building a great business.

Or it may be the writing and performing of a hit song. Political office. Becoming a respected and well known chef. Becoming a doctor, or a painter, or a renowned writer. Maybe you want to build a house or become the best salesperson in your field. This is something that should speak to your core ambitions and it's well known that your chances for success will largely be in direct relation to the passion you have for this goal. Remember when you have endless curiosity for a topic or a discipline the reading and research will not be effortless but it will be easier.

"Believe you can and you're halfway there."

Theodore Roosevelt 1858-1919

And don't forget to inspire the release of the great motivator dopamine by consciously celebrating every accomplishment along the way. It will fuel your efforts, add enjoyment and draw you on to the next goal to accomplish along the journey.

And if you're a notoriously pessimistic person when it comes to your ambitions? That's okay. Don't worry about it, do something about it. Weaken the neural pathways of pessimism by repeating positive affs day after day, day in and day out. The positives will soon become the pathways of choice as the negatives will begin to fade. How?

Because you're not allowing yourself to tread those mental paths over and over though this might take effort and time. After all, you've literally myelinated/lubricated them with consistent use. Be mindful and persistent and pave a different path that will lead you to success with the power of auto-suggestion. Your bright future, that one with you actually living your dream, depends on it.

When you're thinking an empowering aff and you get a mental burst of chemistry in the form of dopamine, serotonin and more your thought's neural connections are brighter and more intense. This heightens the impact of the thought on your subconscious, and by repeating this thought one anchors it into thought loops, memories of success, memories of good feeling. As it becomes a habit you will be a living breathing example of the truth that every thought you think changes you. But now you're taking the process to a different, more profound level. And here's where you will really see and feel the difference as you march confidently down the line achieving goal after goal.

This is why it's important to employ a *"seek and select"* method of finding those affs most likely to produce this effect and thus continue the process of changing your mental attitude for the better. It's a growing thing and just as the seed you plant in the spring grows into a verdant and fruit bearing plant by harvest time you, too, will witness the power of harnessing your thoughts and becoming more focused in the pursuit of your dream.

We're all familiar with the *"trial and error"* method of seeking a solution to a challenge. Let's alter that descriptive phrase and make it *"trial and triumph"*. We'll try affs and really use the repetition of auto-suggestion to establish new neural pathways to success. And sometimes we'll find, through trial and triumph, that line that truly speaks to your psyche in such a way that your limbic brain will reward you with a feeling that you're on the right pathway to changing the way you think and yes, this will be the pathway to success.

I wish I'd figured this out way back when as that would have been the ideal time to start this, but I didn't. So the next best time to leverage this realization? Right now. Just think it and eventually it will come to be. Employ those affs that speak to what's holding you back. You'll know, you'll feel when you're on the right track and when you are? Barrel down that thought line until it's well worn and you've established it as a vital part of who you are, the person in control and in command. And this person on a mission is going places.

So don't worry about tomorrow. Focus on today and the thoughts you wisely choose in this moment and tomorrow, my friend, will take care of itself. We are the product of those that came before us, those that found ways to protect and project their DNA into the next generation. You are the pinnacle of success at life's most fundamental urge, survival, springing from that limbic system wrapped in that giant cortex. And thank those who kept your gene pool alive and thriving, their persistence and strength delivered you to your life.

You have the opportunity to take that level of success and before you die accomplish all that you can. You've been given the chance to make your future brighter and all you have to do is brighten the present a bit with better, more empowering and enlightening thought. And the exciting fact is that the power to accomplish this lies right between your ears. Use that power and train your brain to serve you and thus all future generations for one person's elevation is indeed at a most profound level the elevation of your tribe and our entire species.

And while you repeat your chosen affs, with feeling, remember that great success can be a lonely outpost. Aglitter with prosperity, sure, but without your social network be it family or friends, an empty victory. Your overall life satisfaction is dependent on balance. So seek that balance, have some fun, and save time for solitude and solid, refreshing sleep. And eat well for both enjoyment and to feed your body and your brain what it truly needs to survive and thrive.

Every day in every way I am seeking a balanced, enjoyable life full of love.

Every day in every way Dan, you are seeking a balanced, enjoyable life full of love.

Every day in every way Dan is seeking a balanced, enjoyable life full of love.

I am a genius applying my wisdom to having fun!

Dan, you are a genius applying your wisdom to having fun!

Dan Wedin is a genius applying his wisdom to having fun!

Keep in mind that success is all about your ability to adapt and your ability to adapt is rooted in your ability to change. You've already experienced this as you came through life and experienced the epiphanies that inevitably arrive, along with the resulting exultant brain chemistry as you learn new things and grow. The secret sauce of success is in your incorporation and respect for your ability to change.

Stop when you resist change that you know is good for you. Stop when you spurn the opportunity to learn something new that you are curious about. Seek and ye shall find, yes, but direct that seeking intelligently toward those things that will fuel you along the path toward your dream.

When you acquire new knowledge you'll sense the flow of neural chemistry that will feel good. And when you do something intelligent such as this that will spur brain chemistry and this will encourage you to return to this behavior again and again. Trust your instincts and make every day your opportunity to think, grow and advance.

I can remember myself at an earlier age when I was pathetically ignorant about so very much. And a semblance of that person still exists within me. But in the process of overcoming that ignorance, often via the intensely valuable and at times painful method of real world experience, one gets the cue that this is indeed one's life work. To *"plumb the depths of one's ignorance"* and move confidently step by step, thought by thought, to a new and better tomorrow.

That tomorrow is awaiting your arrival. Take great care of this day and your chances for a greater tomorrow suddenly improve dramatically.

The past is history, the future's a mystery and they call it the present as it's a gift.

Unknown; Attributable to Alice Morse Earle, perhaps, see below.

"The clock is running. Make the most of today. Time waits for no man. Yesterday is history. Tomorrow is a mystery. Today is a gift. That's why it is called the present."

Alice Morse Earle, 1851-1911

"Yesterday is relative, tomorrow is speculative, but today is electric. That's why it's called current."

Travis Dultz, 2015

"Yesterday's the past, tomorrow's the future, and today's a GIFT. That's why they call it the present."

Bill Keane, Family Circle, 1994

"Many people will walk in and out of your life, but only true friends will leave footprints in your heart. To handle yourself, use your head; To handle others, use your heart. Anger is only one letter short of danger. If someone betrays you once, it is his fault; if he betrays you twice, it is your fault. Great minds discuss ideas; average minds discuss events; small minds discuss people. He who loses money, loses much; he, who loses a friend, loses much more; he, who loses faith, loses all. Beautiful young people are accidents of nature, but beautiful old people are works of art. Learn from the mistakes of others. You can't live long enough to make them all yourself. Friends, you and me....You brought another friend....And then there were 3....We started our group....Our circle of friends....And like that circle....There is no beginning or end....Yesterday is history. Tomorrow is mystery. Today is a gift."

Eleanor Roosevelt, 1884-1962

Now is the time. *Indeed.*

You Are A GENIUS

It's not where you are, it's the state you're in.

Chapter Eleven
The Third Person

In the course of utilizing Emil Coue's famous *"Every day in every way..."* line and the *"I am a genius..."* affs I discovered something that may be specific to me. Or not. That is that I occasionally would try the I-You-He lines in reverse order, as singles and out of order completely. This led me to explore how these affected how I feel with each line alone and in groups. And their impact on my subconscious behaviors and the brain chemistry each line inspires.

It turns out for me using the third person, or speaking of myself in a *"self-distancing"* manner seemed to deliver a heightened effect, as I've mentioned. So I plunged deeper into the practice and was startled to note that it was more effective at inspiring the feelings and results I desired than any of the other combinations. Why was that?

That's a good question, but as you may have noted by now I'm more interested in the result than the machinations behind it. It's possible over the course of the next few years critics and readers will weigh in with the psychology behind it and I welcome this further exploration whole-heartedly. I am but a student of the art of thinking and embrace further exploration leading to illumination. Or humiliation, whatever it takes to advance the cause.

When I talk to myself in the third person, something I never do out loud in public, but certainly out loud at times in private, I feel a sensation in my brain that's not present with the first and second person. I suggest you try this as well. It may be a personality trait that I have, and if that's the case, I'm certain there are others who would find this valuable as well. And, like all the other lines, excessive use can dull the impact a bit, moving me to explore other gestations. So it's possible I simply established the first and second persons solidly in my subconscious, and the third person needed some further work, who knows? But for now let's explore the wonders of speaking to oneself in the third person.

Perhaps it's that when talking of myself rather than to myself I'm able to develop a clearer picture of who I am, and who I am becoming or aspiring to become. All I know is it seems to help me solidify whatever concept I'm focused on within my subconscious as I feel it deeply. Try this while inserting your full name in place of mine, of course:

Daniel Burke Wedin is a genius applying his wisdom.

Daniel Burke Wedin is a genius applying his wisdom.

Daniel Burke Wedin is a genius applying his wisdom.

And then try it sincerely while focusing on an area of improvement in your psyche you've identified as needing work:

Daniel Burke Wedin is a genius applying his wisdom to his ability to maintain focus.

Daniel Burke Wedin is a genius applying his wisdom to his ability to maintain focus.

Daniel Burke Wedin is a genius applying his wisdom to his ability to maintain focus.

And in addition to specific areas, as I've noted, I like to fill in the blanks between these efforts with global improvement lines:

Daniel Burke Wedin is a genius applying his wisdom to his life.

Daniel Burke Wedin is a genius applying his wisdom to his life.

Dan Wedin

Daniel Burke Wedin is a genius applying his wisdom to his life.

Then I've also added something to this that seemed to bear fruit in my daily life:

Daniel Burke Wedin is a genius applying his wisdom to his life and his wife.

Daniel Burke Wedin is a genius applying his wisdom to his life and his wife.

Daniel Burke Wedin is a genius applying his wisdom to his life and his wife.

Call me crazy, though you shan't be the first, but this last set of third person only affs and in the first, second and third format seemed to improve my relationship with my wife. Go figure, huh? Relationships that are strong and growing are never just static so acknowledging that one can do better perhaps plants that seed in the subconscious that can grow and flourish.

And let your imagination run free through the dream fields of your subconscious. Where are the trouble spots? Where are the visions of what you desire? What are your challenges on a daily basis? Do you work around them? Stand in denial about them? Give these questions some thought, frame an articulate query and then move on with the thoughts they inspire and the affs that allay them. Affs that perhaps will, over time, weaken their hold and thus allow them to be replaced with more powerful and beneficial thinking and feeling.

And take note of things that strike you on this mental journey. You may be able to begin to assemble the goals which will lead to the achievement of a long-held dream. To begin the process of ridding yourself of low thinking that's holding you back. To change ancient resentments or envious feelings that you can now cut loose from your life and live free of their negative-feeling-producing thoughts. It's all possible but only you can identify those unique characteristics that you must judge as worthy of your existence or as a stain upon it.

And don't worry about having to analyze which works best and which feels flat. Your brain's chemistry will guide you. When you are thinking a thought that has an impact that you can feel is helpful (remember your brain's pre-programmed for survival and sustenance) you may feel a rush of dopamine. It doesn't last long but it provides all the incentive you need to continue the thought until you've squeezed the benefit, for now, out of the practice. You'll automatically return to it, believe me, as we all respond favorably to dopamine, aka, an opioid. It's a fine reward and we like rewards, don't we? Of course we do.

But should you feel what amounts to no response just stick with it. Keep altering your approach or return to Coue's line in all three persons and persist. It's difficult to think of getting better and better every day in every way and not make some progress. But we're individuals and results will vary. Consistency and persistency is key to positioning yourself for success with auto-suggestion.

Daniel Burke Wedin is a genius applying his wisdom to consistently leveraging the power of auto-suggestion.

Daniel Burke Wedin is a genius applying his wisdom to eliminating doubt and fear in the pursuit of his goals.

Daniel Burke Wedin is a genius applying his wisdom to rooting out from his thinking greed, envy, jealousy and resentment.

Daniel Burke Wedin is a genius applying his wisdom to always being in the right place at the right time engaged in the right activity.

There are perhaps as many paths as there are individuals on earth. And the subconscious brain is so vast, so intricate, that it is indeed one of science's last frontiers. So once you've walked this path for a few days or weeks, pay attention to the excitement you feel as a result of a shot of dopamine or other uplifting chemistry with a particular variety of affs.

But the key is to stick with it as the conventional wisdom is that you want to continue something for forty-five days to firmly root it mentally as a good habit. And good habits are our friends, right? You have some already, and no doubt some bad when it comes to thinking. Focusing on the good will weaken the bad until they're simply memories and those we can live with as curiosities from who and where you once were mentally.

If it means you must say these lines with sincerity to yourself or out loud, invest that time. The results will come. It's a journey that's quite interesting in that sometimes gradual changes occur that only reveal themselves over time. One day you wake up with a favored aff coursing through your brain. This is magic and a signal that the thoughts and feelings have blazed a neural pathway that you want to endlessly encourage. This new "code" is being written in that most inscrutable subconscious of yours, gradually improving its focus and upgrading the quality of the thoughts in your main neural pathways.

In my particular case I began in earnest and it was a year in before I even thought about the need to make the affs a habit. It just happened. It's inevitable unless something in your makeup resists and there will no doubt be cases of that. Patience, persistence, and consistent application will be your allies in this effort.

And the payoff is the habit will begin to inspire the release of dopamine, serotonin and oxytocin but in most cases it will be small doses of the first. Dopamine's released when we see something we can acquire that supports our survival and this qualifies in my mind. After all, I was simply trying to get better in an effort to live beyond the "five years" predicted. The doc in the hospital at my bedside had called me the "miracle baby". Okay, I simply wanted to conjure another "miracle" and I encourage you to test the limits of your beliefs.

Think big, think bold, and know that every thought you think changes you in some small way. And occasionally a new thought will burst forth with such a flood of feelings that it can potentially change your life quite dramatically. Think *"epiphany"*. Thoughts are seeds and the harvest of deeds will appear in due season. And remember that boldness has genius, power and magic in it, a thought compliments of our friend, Mr. Goethe.

Maintain a steady thought diet of those affs that address improvement of your entire being, which one might call *"thought adaptogens"*. In the herbal kingdom an adaptogen is something taken to relieve stress, and bring one *"back to the middle"*. The reduction of stress is a noble goal for health and well-being, I think we can all agree on that.

And stress can produce cortisol, which is part of our brain's pharmacy, but when thought patterns and situations overproduce this chemical some very negative things and bad feelings can happen. Cortisol, too, plays a key role in our mammalian instinct to survive, but we don't want to encourage it as a steady diet. Too much can have severely deleterious effects on our health from head to toe.

Cortisol is a product of your adrenal glands (following the actions of other glands) and is a famous element in the "fight or flight syndrome", thus part of our body's intricate defense system. But too much too often can lead to a host of ills including *"Cushing Syndrome"*, just as too little is what's experienced by those suffering from *"Addison's Disease"*. Neither is something any of us would like to experience or encourage so while cortisol performs many valuable functions it's something we want in balance, there when we need it but well regulated under normal circumstances.

It's been reported that the late President Kennedy suffered from Addison's Disease. That fact, in light of his life story, gives me pause. Was his lack of Cortisol influencing the risks he took in WWII, and in his political and personal life? He exhibited a kind of uber-braveness, a coolness and calmness of character and perhaps that might have been influenced by an inhibited natural warning system for danger. Just speculation, but it's an interesting line of thought.

It's been termed the body's alarm system and yes, we need it, but when the alarm stays on our bodies suffer the consequences. Without delving deeper into the details, let's focus on maintaining a calm, balanced perspective with good thoughts that give us what we desire, a calm mind with a heart at rest.

Daniel Burke Wedin is a genius applying his wisdom to maintaining a sense of calm.

Daniel Burke Wedin is a genius applying his wisdom to his calm attitude.

Daniel Burke Wedin is a genius applying his wisdom to calmness of mind.

Daniel Burke Wedin is a genius applying his wisdom to inner calmness.

Every day in every way I maintain a pleasant calmness.

Every day in every way Dan maintains a pleasant calmness.

Every day in every way Dan Wedin maintains a pleasant calmness.

Every day in every way Dan remains exceedingly calm at all times.

Every day in every way Dan remains exceedingly calm at all times.

Every day in every way Dan Wedin remains exceedingly calm at all times.

What works for you? What produces the recognition of the value of calmness and inspires you to seek out that calm peace of mind that you can return to again and again in our often stressful world? Stress is our frenemy, as it were, there to elevate the necessary adrenaline and cortisol so we can escape danger but hopefully we're not positioning ourselves very often for this kind of chemical cycle. It can exhaust you physically and psychologically.

Goals and Dreams in the Third Person

As one might imagine I've used the thoughts in this book to actually produce this book. And that, in itself, has been very instructive. As any writer will attest one can hit dead spots along the way, moments where the inspiration falters and the work becomes, well, work. That leads to lifeless writing so in response to those periods I've homed in on those affs that move me forward returning me to a more productive perch from which to write.

And overall I try to stay true to the original version and I have my Wife to thank for pushing me to begin to put thoughts down in an organized fashion. As I've noted before, I'm often a very disorganized individual and I admire those who seem to lead more ordered existences. So, of course, I've used *"organized"* in a variety of affs to good effect.

So it led me to focus on the topics and the thoughts but also to pay attention to the overall dream of completing the writing and editing and taking it to market so I can be murdered for any number of mistakes. That's okay, I can take it. Life failed me once and while the rescue was an exhilarating experience, I know that inevitably I'll succumb to its fateful arc. I'll take what comes in the meantime blissfully.

Dan Wedin is a genius applying his wisdom to accomplishing those goals necessary to bring his dream to reality.

Dan Wedin is a genius applying his wisdom to reaching the goals he desires to make his dream come true.

Dan Wedin is a genius applying his wisdom achieving his goals one by one until he reaches the realization of his dreams.

Dan Wedin is a genius applying his wisdom to allowing his dreams to come true.

Daniel Burke Wedin is a genius applying his wisdom to accomplish his goals and make his dreams come true more exquisitely than he could imagine.

Dan Wedin is a genius applying his wisdom to the accomplishment of his goals making the realization of his exquisite dreams inevitable.

Find the language that speaks to you, that inspires you, that touches you deeply. And then repeat it to yourself frequently as you go through your days until it feels as if it's lost its impact. Then assess where you are and what your essential needs at that moment might be. Ask yourself what your needs are at that very moment! Then address those needs with your own self-created aff including the basic format. There are no rules, per se, in human thought, but a word of caution.

When I first started this in an organized fashion each day beyond Coue's line, I'd employ the *"I am a genius, applying my wisdom…"* with variations to follow. I found it absolutely exhilarating and perhaps you'll experience some of that. I thought I'd found nirvana! I could feel the euphoric sense created by a release of pleasurable brain chemistry. And the feeling made me aware of the positive impact these feelings had on my health which at the time was a shadow of what it had been.

Over time it seemed to be quite easy to trigger these releases though I did it on an intermittent basis as life tends to provide distractions, does it not? I felt myself getting quite full of myself and since I, like most people, have an aversion to pretentiousness I responded with an aff of my own which was quite effective.

You Are A GENIUS

Daniel Burke Wedin is a genius applying his wisdom to his humility.

Dan Wedin is a genius applying his wisdom to his deep sense of humility.

Dan Wedin is a genius applying his wisdom to cultivate his humble nature.

This worked quite effectively and I marveled at how I could think of humility, I could think of gratitude yet when couched in these terms I found I felt those feelings. That told me that I was indeed having some impact on my subconscious mind at a much deeper level than just turning the term over in my conscious mind. It was the difference between intellectual calculation and emotional exploration.

Think of your subconscious mind as a massive library with information, impressions, videos, photos, art, and unending stories. Think of your conscious mind as the large window next to the entrance with a display shelf just inside. Yes, the window shows a lot, and the view can be changed at a moment's notice. Yet the library behind is much deeper with more histories and memories and all manner of tricks and hidden reading rooms.

If you are to organize this library, and bring its great power to bear in your life then it must be catalogued, organized and the morale of the staff elevated. So by consistent input through the entrance, aka your conscious mind, one is able to thoughtfully choose those affs, those thoughts and let them work their magic.

It's apparent that many of us use our minds and are often abused by the same device. What this book is designed to do is help you willfully select your areas of focus, after all, we have limited time on this earth with which to use this human wonder. As you *"train your brain"* to focus on what you want to be thinking about, in areas in which you desire growth, then by consistently inputting strategic thoughts they become the search engine for the thoughts, feelings and emotions you have chosen. Illuminate the good, the empowering, and deny time and space to that which denigrates you.

In time you'll find the more general affs just springing to mind and in the hustle and bustle of modern life it's a gentle and welcome reminder that you are in control of this, the most powerful data storage and retrieval device in the universe. When I refer to *"general"*, I'm talking about those that address topics such as happiness, love, focus, et cetera.

And of course the more repetition you apply to any particular aff the more likely it is to bounce into your conscious mind unbidden in a thought loop. This is a habit, once attained, that will nurture you, inspire you, and advance you toward all you aspire to be.

"These virtues are formed in man by his doing the actions."

A phrase from Aristotle's Nicomachean Ethics (in this case "virtues" equals the habitual behavior, therefore the virtue itself becomes not a conscious choice, save at first; in practice, by simply thinking the thought with focus, it becomes habitual behavior). This is the conversion of a virtuous, beneficial thought into daily action as it has become involuntary.

"Excellence is an art won by training and habituation: we do not act rightly because we have virtue or excellence, but we rather have these because we have acted rightly... We are what we repeatedly do. Excellence, then, is not an act but a habit."

Will Durant, "The Story of Philosophy"; American writer, philosopher and historian, 1885-1981, in trying to get at the heart of Aristotle's message.

And while you're focusing on the good, on the strong, on the inspirational you'll be ignoring the bad, the weak and the discouraging. This is supplanting, blazing the neural pathways you want to ferociously and consistently encourage while ignoring those neural pathways you seek to see fade into oblivion. They are not who you are, they are just what you happen to focus on currently.

And the more you focus on your chosen thoughts the more this dynamic will work in your favor. You'll be slowly turning the vessel that is you, cultivating the garden of your mind and training your brain to just fly the plane on a wonderfully programmed and dependable autopilot. And the new direction will be one of your own choosing, one that represents your highest aspirations.

So try the Third Person. I'll be curious to see if the trio or one of them becomes the salient force in the lives of others. I use all three, consistently, but spend a good amount of time in the Third Person. There's something quite different to me about it but there is no final conclusion to the story as the quest continues. *For Life.*

You Are A GENIUS

It's not where you are, it's the state you're in.

Chapter Twelve
Brain Nutrition

You are what you eat, right? If that were true I'd be part cheeseburger, part cod-herring-salmon-oyster-clam-crab-shrimp, part steak-ribs-chops and coffee, pizza, green tea, spinach, romaine, beer, kefir, Parmesan and Romano, seltzer water, gin, vodka, beer and wine and much more would be coursing through my bloodstream. But while there's a kernel of truth there I think a more apt statement might be, *"What you eat dictates your future vitality."* And actually, even more to the point we are what we eat after it's been processed by our gut bacteria, aka, microbiome.

Now those are lines of logic I can defend. Live on fast food and sugary pop? You're headed for ill health and a sluggish brain. And you've increased your chance of cognitive failure, i.e., some form of dementia as you age. It's common to read that Alzheimer's springs from a specific gene yet dietary studies over time prove over and over that diet, specifically how much saturated fat rich in Omega-6 fatty acids and sugar you consume, that plays the dominant statistical role.

When I bought a copy of *"Food: Your Miracle Medicine"*, Jean Carper's New York Times bestseller two decades ago, I was already interested in changing my diet to improve my health and mental focus, and this was a springboard. It led me to read *"Your Miracle Brain"*, *"The Anti-Cancer Diet"* and *"Miracle Cures"* as well.

Carper doesn't deal with myths and tales, her work reflects science. For instance, *"Food: Your Miracle Medicine"* is based on ten thousand scientific studies performed at hospitals and universities and published in the New England Journal of Medicine, JAMA (the Journal of the American Medical Association) and Lancet (the British Medical Journal).

For someone studying nutrition it amounted to actionable intelligence. And as a writer and strategist, it made sense to me to select foods and supplements that would leave me most capable of performing at a high level. It was at this time, too, that I discovered how foods affect moods, and that was exciting. I like to be in a good mood, I like inspirational thoughts and music and settings. And I like to be in an excellent frame of mind to just take it all in.

And while I studied nutrition, it didn't always result in my consistently making the right choices. Oh, sure, it impacted my diet but I was in transition and hadn't fully made a commitment to a truly healthy diet based on all I knew. And the reality is I still haven't, but I'm trying. And of course, all I knew was what I had studied and read and some of the assumptions of an earlier age have changed profoundly. This is the hallmark of science.

"It's not what you don't know that gets you into trouble, it's what you know for certain that just ain't so."

Anonymous, though attributed to any number of individuals including Mark Twain, Will Rogers, Artemus Ward and others.

The point is that there is no finality to the term, *"education"*. I contend that it is our ego that points to the sheepskin, the degree, the advanced studies. Yet all of us want to endlessly plumb the dark depths of our ignorance. For what we've learned a decade ago is perhaps moot today. One must learn, question, continue the study, re-learn, re-evaluate, and arrive at new conclusions. That may, over time, be called into question once again. Our knowledge of much, and this includes nutrition and brain science, is a growing, organic entity. There is no endpoint to anyone's *"education"*.

One must continually, habitually question what they *"know"*, and be open to an honest examination of the *"facts"*. In so many things those are actually few and far between. This is the stuff *"shattered myths"* are made of. And this definitely includes the study of what we should be eating for optimal brain empowerment. Yet we've come a long way, haven't we?

Our brains have changed little in thousands of years, yet what we power them with has been altered dramatically in the last few decades. Radical, really, has been the wave of changes to not only our diets but to the way crops are grown, animals are raised and foods are processed. That this massive shift has affected the health of our bodies and brains has not gone unnoticed. The field of "nutritional neuroscience" has exploded with a wealth of knowledge that shows the potential to make us smarter, live longer and lead a more vital existence from birth to the grave.

Sugar's a great example. Our brains were essentially the same as they are today back in the times when we hunted and fished and gathered. Sugar and fat were rare in nature and on consumption produced effects in the brain that signaled that this was a choice, a behavior that we definitely wanted to repeat as they represented energy and satiety on a higher level than those foods with less fat (satiety) and sugar (energy). Of course there was raw honey and that was super-prized, and fatty fish and certain portions of the wild game meats with higher fat content (think rib steak as opposed to round steak) and our brains recorded that accordingly.

So the mechanisms, the evolved responses to these elements are deeply ingrained. Yet as the composition of our diet and the foods that have come to replace those ancient ones has changed, we've paid a heavy price. Even as late as 1900 our sugar consumption was tiny compared to today, with estimates of four pounds then to well over one hundred pounds today. And since sugar signals the brain to hang onto fat our bodies respond accordingly and we can see the obesity epidemic with which we now deal as a species.

Artificial sweeteners are especially pernicious in that they signal the brain that we're consuming something sweet which triggers a release of our available blood sugar to our cells, so what happens? We've tried to fool Mother Nature, haven't we? But she's a step ahead of us so while we're consuming a "pretend sweet, or artificial sweetener" and it triggers the "real sweet" response. This leaves us with lower blood sugar which makes us "hangry", and this of course spurs us to eat and studies show that we actually end up consuming more than if we'd just used regular sugar. Vicious cycle, isn't it? And another demonstration that sooner or later Mother Nature will have her way, despite our efforts at deception.

The effects of just our overconsumption of sugar are widespread and deadly. The brain is especially susceptible to this damage in the form of overproduction of a thing called "AGEs", or "advanced glycosylation end products". These AGEs are sugar-damaged proteins which turn yellowish-brown and they accelerate the aging of bones, joints, blood vessels and the brain, causing damage as dangerous as the notorious oxygen-free radicals. And AGEs double down on damage by producing free radicals on their own. There's no question, limiting your sugar intake and fructose intake can be a healthy choice to make.

The more sugar you consume the more AGEs found in your bloodstream. This can lead to the diabetic nerve damage known as "neuropathy". Research is showing that this process, known as "glycation" is a driver behind the deterioration of brain cells which can produce neurodegenerative diseases and that includes Alzheimer's and possibly even the memory loss we associate with aging.

I'm no nutritional expert (that should be underscored!) but even my cursory research indicates with some certainty that to protect the brain for one's entire life sugar is to be limited way beyond what's considered normal in our plush culinary era. Also, "Alpha-Lipoic Acid" has been identified in doses of 300-600 milligrams daily as a means of helping prevent diabetes and its myriad complications including neuropathy.

You may want to consider consulting your doctor or nutritionist for guidance. But in the interest of protecting and preserving your vital brain functions, a little sugar goes a long way. And a healthy diet contains enough for your brain's needs, so cue the richly colorful berry kingdom here, with a starring role for blueberries which are key to brain health. I eat them almost daily.

And we're lucky enough here in the Northwest to enjoy a probiotic-rich kefir from Nancy's Dairy in Eugene, Oregon and it comes in blueberry. I've also consumed the Life Way brand and it's good, though not quite as probiotic-rich. The number of healthful bacteria in this product is astounding, though, in both cases and they're also delicious. One prime brain food as we discover more and more about the link via the vagus nerve between our brain and our microbiome. Some even refer to it as our "second brain".

For more information about Nancy's visit nancysyogurt.com

Now let's look at Omega-3 and Omega-6 fatty acids. In the not-too-distant past our diets left us with a nearly equal ratio. Today most of us have a preponderance of Omega-6 streaming through our systems and the damage this imbalance has created is nearly immeasurable. From joint deterioration, memory loss, brain cell inflammation to the actual loss of brain cells, warped nerve cell membranes, interference with neuronal message transmission, to strokes, Alzheimer's, and nearly all degenerative brain diseases.

When Omega-6 fatty acids are dominant over Omega-3's, all hell breaks loose in the brain. We literally handicap ourselves mentally and physically and create a society with the wherewithal to be the healthiest in history but facing the reality of ill health and disease all around us. We eat way more Omega-6's these days, and estimates run as high at fifteen times as much as Omega-3's. Yet our bodies are designed for balance in this area, and the imbalance costs us dearly in quality of life and medical bills. And brain functioning.

Omega-3's are brain builders and play a role in mood as well. Populations consuming the most fish and seafood are less prone to depression. A quick look around the world tells one that Omega-3 rich diets lead to happier, healthier populations. We've literally gone the wrong direction and it's not hard to see why. The American food industry is a mass production wonder, but it's driven by competing forces and the drive to lower costs and raise profit margins means the use of Omega-6 oils and fats dominates. And the artificially low prices of our protein staples such as beef, pork and chicken due to feed subsidies means we consume meat, yes, but critically not the meat of our ancestors.

In the early days of civilization populations centered near bodies of water, be it the ocean, lakes, streams or inland seas. So we consumed vast quantities of seafood and when we hunted and killed animals that were foragers, not corn and grain eaters, their Omega-3 content was high, just as it is today for grass fed animals.

This Omega-3 rich diet led to a massive increase in the size of our cerebral cortex, and that evolution has produced who we are today.

We're killing ourselves with knives and forks which in plastic form are even more deadly due to the foods they're associated with. But each one of us is actually very fortunate when it comes to nutrition. We live in an age of almost unbelievable plenty. The choices in an average grocery store are staggering. If we make the decision to eat for health, and specifically brain health, that store is our oyster and we the pearl. And don't underestimate the oyster when it comes to brain health. Seriously.

Once I ordered a few dozen of the briny mollusks from Willapa Bay up the coast in Washington. I'd specified two day delivery but since I was working at home I was very excited when the very next day the UPS truck pulled up. It was eleven in the morning and from my office window I could see the driver walking toward the door with my order. The Willapa is the source of something like a quarter of the nation's fresh supply and I'd ordered Willapa's and Kumamoto's. I could taste them!

I quickly opened the box and then the styrofoam container with the ice and bivalves. I got out a cutting board and my Danielson oyster knife and popped the top of one of the prized gems. I stared at the clear flesh surrounded by the delightful nectar, noting the condition which was perfect in the late fall. I raised the oyster to my lips and tipped all of the contents into my waiting mouth.

It was perfect! In seconds I involuntarily found myself in my socks on my tip-toes with arms extended upward in the Pride Pose. I didn't even know what it was at the time. But later I was studying foods and their effect on mood and discovered that selenium has a mood elevating impact on the brain. Further research indicated that oysters are rich in this mineral. And since oysters are so easily digested and I wondered if it was possible that some of that selenium either in the oyster or the "nectar" in which it was bathed might have produced that involuntary and joyous reaction.

They're also rich in tyrosine, another mood elevator and precursor of dopamine. Though I knew there was also an element of the elation one associates with victory, with winning as a hunter-gatherer might celebrate a choice find. These little calcium-carbonate encased gems certainly qualified so that no doubt played a role as well.

So if you're interested in optimal brain function today and a lifetime that maintains that state, eat a diet with a generous component of fatty fish such as wild salmon and Monterey Bay Aquarium approved farmed salmon, herring, sardines, and other fatty fish. Consider quality fish oil supplements if you're not a fish eater or find it difficult to locate or too expensive. Twenty-five years ago I visited a naturopath while dealing with the after-effects of a nine month stint on antibiotics, as I've noted. I know, bad idea, but I really didn't understand the implications at the time. She put me on fish oil capsules, a quality probiotic and yogurt and had me tamp down the bread and beer consumption of which I was so fond.

The fact of the matter is our brains would not have developed such a large cortex on top of our limbic system were it not for the incredible brain building properties of our ancient Omega-3 rich and natural diet. So should we really be messing with Mother Nature again here? Or should we let what historically built and maintained our brain with modern day flourishes?

I contend we should focus on assembling the best diet we can for our health and the health of our brains. An hour spent searching the web for great source material on this topic will be an hour that will pay off, for life. And what's an hour or two per week? And I never stop plumbing the depths of my ignorance when it comes to my diet and nutrition and how to make it ever more intriguing and interesting and delicious.

Food can be a wonderful source of exhilarating brain chemistry based on its content, appearance and taste and texture. Why not? We're an evolving species so it makes sense to use that dynamic in our daily life to grow ever more healthy and vital with optimal brain function. And to me it's just a lot of fun which I put a high premium on due to its impact on not just my level of satisfaction with life but also its profound impact on brain development. Any time you can experience and taste something new and different you literally grow your brain by blazing new neural pathways and what happens in your brain today presages your future. Use it or lose it is not just a cliché when it comes to the brain, it's a fact.

It's not the number of brain nerve cells, or neurons you have, the average brain has 86 billion, what's more important is the activity within the brain and the quality of the neural pathways your life's experiences and thoughts have built. This is where our nature as individuals really demonstrates its uniqueness. And this is why we all react somewhat differently to the same stimuli.

Your established and well-worn neural pathways are almost irresistible and that's a positive and a negative element in our development. If the pathways of choice are strong, empowering thoughts and reactions you think like a strong, empowered individual. If one's brain's most used neural pathways are timid and fearful and self-defeating then it's not hard to see how the same stimuli would produce a completely different reaction.

So nutrition and the health of your brain is important in using "You Are A Genius" and its techniques. But equally important are the thoughts you choose to encourage as if one perseveres those become the main thoroughfares of your daily reactions, reflections and actions. But if you suffer from brain fog you can see that training your brain is like training for a marathon when you're in ill health. It just doesn't work.

So eat for enjoyment but include fatty fish or fish oil, a variety of colorful berries and fruits and lots of leafy green vegetables. And don't forget our friends in the cruciferous vegetable family including broccoli, cabbage, cauliflower and Brussels sprouts. We have the opportunity to dine on a diet similar to our ancestors yet with a huge advantage in variety. Leverage that for your brain and your overall health. After all, if you're not feeling good you've a much tougher challenge in thinking clearly and focusing on anything other than the aches and pains and other symptoms.

What are some great brain foods? How about kippered snacks, Brunswick is a good brand. Blueberries are the only thing known to man to rebuild brain cells and Trader Joe's sells a "Boreal" version of lowbush (highest in antioxidants) blueberries picked in the wild above the Arctic Circle. They are as inky blue as they are delicious and a perfect addition to plain yogurt.

Salmon lox is also good but I'd avoid varieties preserved with nitrates and nitrites. Fresh wild salmon is excellent and for guidance do rely on the Monterey Bay Aquarium's seafood lists which come conveniently in individual state versions.

Leafy green vegetables including spinach are excellent. Try washed spinach in a stockpot set to medium, then let it cook down to about an inch and dress with extra virgin olive oil (the real stuff, lots of phonies out there as detailed in "Extra Virgin: The Sublime and Scandalous World of Olive Oil"; one great book by the engaging writer, Tom Mueller) and good Parmesan cheese. Or just weave it into salads or use as a last minute addition to soups.

And try balling up a bunch and holding it with one hand on a cutting board while shaving off thin slices until done. This is a rough form of "chiffonading" and the crinkly little strips make a great garnish and can be added to many different dishes.

Always opt for organic whenever you can. If you're unable to buy organic make sure you wash your fruits and vegetables thoroughly. And develop the habit of subscribing to quality newsletters on nutrition. I've been a mercola.com subscriber for decades and Carper's books are excellent, though now a bit dated. There's an unending treasure trove of information and as you read and study you'll undoubtedly come across inconsistencies and contradictions so opt for those sources that are impartial, not industry-generated, and based on science. *To your Brain Health!*

You Are A GENIUS

It's not where you are, it's the state you're in.

Chapter Thirteen
Final Thoughts on Thought

There are many paths to self-improvement, that much is clear. We're literally surrounded by books, articles, online training programs, mentorship programs; but the most important path is what you choose to think. Without question you have the mental capacity, the strength and the ability to forge new habits through empowered thinking. And as the old knight in the "Last Adventure" advised Indiana Jones, *"Choose wisely."* And that's excellent advice.

If you're faithful daily to the basics, you'll be myelinating neural pathways by igniting electrical impulses with focus and intensity and emotion. This will spur the coating of those neurons along that route not only delivering highly skilled thinking but also inspiring the timing that's so key to an important talent.

These are the basics:

I am a genius applying my wisdom to my Life.

Dan, you are a genius applying your wisdom to your Life.

Dan Wedin is a genius applying his wisdom to his Life.

Every day in every way I'm getting better and better.

Every day in every way, Dan, you are getting better and better.

Every day in every way Dan Wedin is getting better and better.

I am a genius applying my wisdom to my optimal health.

Dan, you are a genius applying your wisdom to your optimal health.

Dan Wedin is a genius applying his wisdom to his optimal health.

Every day in every way I embrace empowering thoughts.

Every day in every way, Dan, you embrace empowering thoughts.

Every day in every way Dan Wedin embraces empowering thoughts.

Beyond these basics, there are endless thought pathways one wants to build based on their own unique circumstances, desires and needs. Yet it's important to work on the basics to establish those well-myelinated neural pathways that will serve you for the rest of your life. And you'll know when this is occurring or has occurred. The thoughts will come to you any time you're of a conscious mind. This is magic, this is supplanting useless thought, and this is setting you on a course for a more successful life.

So once this base of empowering thought has been firmly established the excitement begins. Now you can shore up those weaknesses which you'll face without fear or denial as now you have the means to overcome deficiencies in your own character. And I urge you to pay attention to your character. Build pathways allied with honesty and integrity. Build pathways with compassion and empathy. Build pathways of love for yourself and everything in your life.

I may have given short shrift to the Stoic concept of Amor Fati. Let's not overlook (myself included) the profound value of loving every single aspect of your life. The good, the bad, the ugly, the sorrowful, the tragic, the regrettable; and pay close attention to those times where you admit that you were not acting on behalf of your big self, your self-respecting self, and your kind self.

I've been a warrior at times in my life. I've seen myself battling what I perceived as the forces of evil and sometimes those forces were within my psyche, and within my heart. The work continues. But I've seen examples of different modi operandi that intrigue me, and one is my wife's. When she found herself dealing with conniving troublemakers at work she described the incidents and the sequence of events I'd offer unsolicited advice (which when it comes my way I call it *"the least welcome gift in Western Civilization"*) she'd patiently listen and then explain her modus operandi: Kill them with kindness.

At first I thought this was so Pollyannaish as to be just a weak way of avoiding a confrontation. Yet over time I've come to realize that she didn't give in to the lizard brain and its adrenal excretions as I did. She maintained a placid demeanor and took what I now realize is the high road. And a much less confrontational and effective method of defusing the power the mean, small and petty often wield. I now try, at times with some success, to be an example of her philosophy.

I count it as a victory which of course calls for celebration. A toast to *"Killing them with Kindness."* Clink! And why not? It spares one the stress which confrontational behavior inevitably engenders. And I'm not interested in unnecessary stress at this point in my journey. The world provides all of the stress one might want to experience, don't you think? Stress and the resulting cortisol release is a great defense mechanism when living in the wild but in excess in this civilized world it's not a good habit, it's a bad habit. And habits can be supplanted, as we've seen. If your life currently contains too much stress, try this:

I am a genius applying my wisdom to limiting stress in my life.

Dan, you are a genius applying my wisdom to limiting stress in my life.

Dan Wedin is a genius applying his wisdom to limiting stress in his life.

Every day in every way I exert a wholesome control over the stress in my life.

Every day in every way Dan you exert a wholesome control over stress in your life.

Every day in every way Dan Wedin exerts a wholesome control over stress in his life.

I am a genius applying my wisdom to my calmness and self-control.

Dan, you are a genius applying your wisdom to your calmness and self-control.

Dan Wedin is a genius applying his wisdom to your calmness and self-control.

Every day in every way I enjoy my calmness of mind.

Every day in every way Dan, you enjoy your calmness of mind.

Every day in every way Dan Wedin enjoys his calmness of mind.

I am a genius applying my wisdom to getting better and better every day.

Dan, you are a genius applying your wisdom to getting better and better every day.

Dan Wedin is a genius applying his wisdom to getting better and better every day.

I am a genius applying my wisdom to making everything work out more exquisitely than I ever imagined.

Dan, you are a genius applying your wisdom to making everything work out more exquisitely than you ever imagined.

Dan Wedin

Dan Wedin is a genius applying his wisdom to making everything more exquisitely than he ever imagined.

I am a genius applying my wisdom to succeeding in all that I do.

Dan, you are a genius applying your wisdom to succeeding in all that you do.

Dan Wedin is a genius applying his wisdom to succeeding in all that he does.

I am a genius applying my wisdom to making my life better every day in every way.

Dan, you are a genius applying your wisdom to making your life better every day in every way.

Dan Wedin is a genius applying his wisdom to making his life better every day in every way.

I am a genius applying my wisdom to achieving the highest level of immune response possible.

Dan, you are a genius applying your wisdom to achieving the highest level of immune response possible.

Dan Wedin is a genius applying his wisdom to achieving the highest level of immune response possible.

And one final note on something of great value my Father taught me which he lived:

I am a genius applying my wisdom to never looking up to or down on anyone.

Dan, you are a genius applying your wisdom to never looking up to or down on anyone.

Dan Wedin is a genius applying his wisdom to never looking up to or down on anyone.

And I want to reiterate that one's personal creativity can play a profound role in how they approach the development of the affs they choose to repeat. One can just use the ones I've illuminated, of course, but I think there's tremendous value in choosing those topics that speak to your state of mind and where you are in life. If you're a student like me improving your learning skills helps quantify your comprehension and retention.

I am a genius applying my wisdom to maximizing my learning skills.

Dan, you are a genius applying your wisdom to maximizing your learning skills.

Dan Wedin is a genius applying his wisdom to maximizing his learning skills.

Every day in every way I'm becoming a better researcher.

Every day in every way Dan you're becoming a better researcher.

Every day in every way Dan Wedin's becoming a better researcher.

I also want to emphasize again the value of the "ignition" of the myelination process of a neural pathway which creates a skill. Without this ignition the myelination is not triggered and thus the skill isn't captured or isn't augmented as well as it should be. I've found that occasionally a thought will occur to me, often while driving, that is inspirational so I'll automatically convert it to an aff.

The reason this is so effective at creating that "ignition state" is that it's top of mind and it's important. Thus the aff lifts it from random thought and converts it to a focused one and these often come with an inspiring feeling. Think good brain chemistry and this is the magic that powers the myelination process. Don't treat this lightly, it's the key to your success in this process.

This is exciting as you can feel the physical and mental effect. Ride that wave for as long as that effect continues, even if it begins to recede over time. Milk it for all it's worth. The dopamine release this inspires will fuel further efforts and trust me, you'll get better and better and more proficient at this over time. Stay with it, nurture it, encourage it and make it yours.

And as you read this last chapter if you're feeling a bit overwhelmed remember the automaticity factor. Consistent application of these techniques will soon firmly embed them in your daily thoughts. Just begin with focus, with an earnest nature and with all of the emotion you can muster. The more you can inspire that all-important ignition the more successful you'll be at myelinating those neural pathways. Once that process has been achieved these thoughts and the resulting encouraging feelings and actions will just be part of your life. A very valuable part of your life.

It's not how fast you can adopt these lines, it's not how hard you practice, though both factors help you. It's really that consistency of persistency that truly matters. And I know, I'm playing with words again there. I used to get chided at the table for playing with my food, too. As long as I had armies of lima beans facing off I could avoid eating them.

Stick with it until the thought loops arising from your subconscious rise like blooming flowers in a well-tended garden while you're doing something completely different. Let them rise and shine and crowd out the useless weed seeds of thought to which we're all subject. And the good news is you don't have to weed this garden, just keep planting the good and the bad will soon be supplanted. The world is full of useless weed seeds and overgrowths, yet the garden of your mind is in your control and that's where your mental gardener's efforts should be focused. You really only think, with focus, one thought at a time. Think good thoughts!

If you ever have a recurring thought that doesn't make you feel good identify it, focus on it, and then contemplate an aff that will supplant it. It feels great to disarm an internally generated foe and replace it with a thought ally. And we all need and benefit from thought allies.

Deeply Embedding Thoughts

At some point in this exciting process an interesting phenomenon will present itself, though it can be a subtle yet profoundly important force. The thoughts you've wisely chosen to think on a consistent basis will move from conscious ideas to deeply embedded feelings. This is where true long term mental changes occur in your vast subconscious mind.

Gone will be the need to counteract the near-constant stream of negative thoughts and feelings and you'll perhaps experience a sense of wonder at the fact that your mindset has fundamentally shifted. For the good and for good. Let this knowledge spur you on as you penetrate your conscious and subconscious being with the empowering thoughts that will vault you onward and upward.

So continue the work. With an estimated fifty to a hundred thousand thoughts coursing through one's consciousness daily, and a large share of them being negative, it's important to stay vigilant and focus your chosen thoughts on those areas of your life where you feel the need for improvement is the greatest.

And the interesting thing is that internalizing these thoughts during the course of your hours awake interrupts very few of those thousands of thoughts streaming endlessly. Though I contend the content of those thoughts with this practice over time improves their quality, and combined with questions which call on your subconscious for answers, you'll gain mental wealth and power that may surprise you.

You won't become Einstein overnight, you'll never become Einstein. That is, unless you have a passion for math and science on a world class level but even then, we're talking about Einstein. But that's not the point. The objective is simply to begin and sustain a journey of constant improvement and growth.

You'll feel the results mentally in more orderly thinking, more accelerated growth and results in the pursuits of your goals and dreams that will fuel further efforts. And all that's good, but to me the most important effect is in the moment and it's in the moment that you'll savor the improvement in and the control over your moods. And for me it fuels my creativity which sustains me.

"All children are artists. The problem is how to remain an artist once he grows up."

Picasso 1881-1973 (Officially "Pablo Diego José Francisco de Paula Juan Nepomuceno Cipriano de la Santísima Trinidad Ruiz Picasso")

We get very comfortable with the ebb and flood our moods and mentalities. It's easy to accept states of mind when we feel, hey, that's just me! Make sure that state is one where you're content and enjoy peace of mind, something all of the money in the world cannot buy. And depression is a wide-ranging human condition and if you suffer from this or what you think might be depression, get screened. See your doctor or other health practitioner for the myriad ways modern medicine treats these maladies. Just taking action of any kind puts you on the road to recovery or at least feeling better. Just keep an open mind to the possibilities and explore what your subconscious, think gut feelings, convey to you.

Research natural cures as we live in an age where a wealth of information exists concerning foods and plants and their effect on how we feel. Man has been using a wealth of beneficial plants the world over for eons. Some work, some are hype, some are worthy of further research. Explore, ask questions, consult the experts. I believe in eating for pleasure, but I also get great pleasure out of eating strategically.

If you launch an effort it takes very little time and very few adjustments to make great strides. Ten minutes per day equals nine hours of solid research and education in one short year. An hour per week is fifty-two hours per year. Two and you're at one-hundred and four. And never underestimate how truly short our years are. As I noted, there are times in one's life when we become fully aware that the days might be long but the years are short.

And if you understand and embrace the concept of *"getting better every day in every way"* you come to understand that this affords you nearly endless opportunities for improvement. That's a lot of opportunities so seize them and dedicate yourself to getting better every day in every way and that means in all areas of your life.

And remember that the most important things in life such as love, compassion, empathy, understanding, romance, pleasure, health, fun and yes, money, are not entities in some zero sum game. They hold the power of endless expansion. More for someone else does not mean less for you. Just as more for you does not signal less for someone else. Work to perceive that which feels lacking in your life and design an aff specifically to spur growth in that area. Try these and though I'm writing them in the third person, use the first, second, third format or the one that seems to ignite something mentally for you:

Dan Wedin is a genius applying his wisdom to allowing more love into his life than he could imagine before.

Dan Wedin is a genius applying his wisdom to allowing more compassion into his life than he could imagine before.

Dan Wedin is a genius applying his wisdom to allowing more empathy into his life than he could imagine before.

Dan Wedin is a genius applying his wisdom to allow more understanding into his life than he could imagine before.

Dan Wedin is a genius applying his wisdom to allowing more romance into his life than he could imagine before.

Dan Wedin

Dan Wedin is a genius applying his wisdom to allowing more pleasure into his life than he could imagine before.

Dan Wedin is a genius applying his wisdom to allowing greater health into his life than he could imagine before.

Dan Wedin is a genius applying his wisdom to allowing his immune system to become stronger than he could imagine before.

Dan Wedin is a genius applying his wisdom to allowing more fun into his life than he could imagine before.

Dan Wedin is a genius applying his wisdom to allowing more money into his life than he could imagine before.

Dan Wedin is a genius applying his wisdom to allowing more success into his life than he could imagine before.

Dan Wedin is a genius applying his wisdom to allowing more prosperity into his life than he could imagine before.

Dan Wedin is a genius applying his wisdom to allowing more abundance into his life than he could imagine before.

So there you go. I wish you the best in improving your thinking and your life. I have great faith that this path upon which I tread is one that can hold great value for you, whatever your goals and dreams in life might be. How wonderful it will be if you hold a deep belief in your ability to get better every day in every way!

Just remember, *"There is no joy in life like serving others."* Imagine a world where we all lived by this credo and then became that change as every day in every way you and those around you thought ever more empowering thoughts. Imagine the human force that would produce!

"We don't see things as they are; we see them as we are."

Anais Nin, 1903-1977

To your Health! *And to your ever-improving Thoughts and Life!*

You Are A GENIUS

It's not where you are, it's the state you're in.

Acknowledgments

There are so many to whom I owe a great debt of gratitude for helping me ponder the purpose and tone of "You Are A Genius" but none more than my lovely Wife, Sandra. Her support, her impressions, her encouragement and her timely questions spurred me on and helped me complete this book. Thank You, Dear.

Quite amazing how many assisted me with no idea what was going through my head as we spoke and interacted. I continue to "plumb the depths of my ignorance" and I have no sense that modus operandi will ever change. A toast to All of You!

www.ingramcontent.com/pod-product-compliance
Lightning Source LLC
Chambersburg PA
CBHW051725040426
42447CB00008B/979